Unless Recalled Earlier
DATE DUE

MAR 1 0 1999	
APR - 2 1999	
APR 2 8 1999	

Network Television News

Conviction, Controversy, and a Point of View

Paul C. Simpson

as told to

Patricia G. Lane

and

F. Lynne Bachleda

LEGACY COMMUNICATIONS
Franklin, Tennessee

Hardcover edition ISBN 1-880-692-24-4

Trade paperback edition ISBN 1-880-692-23-6

LEGACY COMMUNICATIONS
P.O. Box 680365
Franklin, Tennessee 37068-0365

TABLE OF CONTENTS

On August 5, 1995, the Vanderbilt Television News Archive in Nashville, Tennessee, entered its twenty-seventh year of videotaping the nightly network news and selected special news programs. Although other partial collections of news programming exist elsewhere, the Vanderbilt University collection remains the world's most extensive and complete archive of television news.

The Archive's collection is open to anyone. For further information about the VTNA's collection and policies, contact:

The Vanderbilt Television News Archive

Suite 704, 110 21st Avenue South

Nashville, TN 37203

Voice 615-322-2927 Fax 615-343-8250

Internet World Wide Web http:/tvnews.Vanderbilt.edu/1

INTRODUCTION

A mong the major sources of news in the United States, television has clearly had the dominant influence, at least since the 1960s. As our world becomes increasingly fast-paced, more and more people rely primarily on television rather than newspapers and magazines for their knowledge about national and international affairs. Poll after poll has shown that network television news has been considered one of the most powerful influences in the United States. In fact, during the 1960s, 1970s, and 1980s, polls showed that leaders in our country ranked the power of network television news second only to that of the Presidency, and Walter Cronkite was often referred to as the second most powerful person in the United States.

Most Americans have given little thought to the powerful influence television exerts on our lives and our country. Many people tend to accept what is reported to them in the national media as complete and factually correct. In many cases, however, what we read and hear is colored by the beliefs and attitudes of the person reporting the story as well as the beliefs and attitudes of his or her employers. Human error and personal opinion can undoubtedly enter into every article we read in the newspaper with our morning cup of coffee, every report we hear on the radio as we drive into work, and every story we watch on the evening news as we settle down in front of the television after a hard day.

Because television in particular has such a vast impact on American society, it would be wise for viewers to constantly remember the ingredients Fred Friendly, former President of CBS News, and Edward R. Murrow believed were necessary for a successful television news program: "conviction, controversy, and a point of view." In a 1967 book entitled *Due to Circumstances Beyond Our Control*..., Friendly explains how he and Murrow, a pioneer and strong influence in the early years of network news, made the transition from the "Hear It Now" radio program to the "See It Now" television program. On the second page of the book, Friendly writes, "... for the most part we were, as Ed said, just a bunch of old radio hands learning the hard way that cameras need something more than emulsion and light valves to create electronic journalism. The missing ingredients were conviction, controversy and a point of view."

Network television news has been including these ingredients ever since, and we must think carefully about what this has meant and continues to mean for our country. We must ask ourselves whose "convictions" and "point of view" are being presented and recognize that one of the primary reasons a story is presented in a particular way is to create "controversy."

It was my belief in the late 1960s, when I first became heavily involved in studying network news programs, that their emphasis on controversy was a major reason controversy began tearing our country apart. It is my belief today that this emphasis over the past thirty years has led our country to an even more dangerous situation.

I founded the Vanderbilt Television News Archive in August of 1968, after learning that the networks erased the news programs after two weeks and that nowhere in the country were actual videotaped recordings of the news programs available for study. I wondered how we could possibly have the second most powerful force in the nation unavailable for study by the American people. Suppose everything the President of the United States did was erased two weeks after he did it and could never be studied by historians, scholars, and the American public. Yet here was an institution second in power only to the Presidency, and no one could ever again see what they had broadcast into the homes of people all over the country. I felt it was critical that this powerful influence be made widely available for study.

At this time, there was beginning to be widespread concern about how television portrayed the events of our world, particularly because of the Vietnam War coverage. As an article in the July 15, 1968, issue of *U. S. News & World Report*, entitled "Television Comes Under Fire," pointed out: "Military commanders often say that television coverage of the war in Vietnam has been one-sided and distorted, and that it has done much to influence opinion at home and abroad in opposition to that war effort." The same article reports on the concern of President Lyndon B. Johnson, members of the Federal Communications Commission, and others about the growing social and political impact of television on the lives and opinions of Americans.

When I began working on this book in the summer of 1994, I intended it to be a history of the founding of the Archive and its first seventeen years of operation, during which I served as volunteer administrative consultant. My primary concern was to show how the Archive was established in the face of strident opposition from the networks, particularly CBS. Naturally, a part of this history involved the history of television coverage itself during those years. As I went through my files and read some of the papers I had written over the years, comparisons with the current situation in our country kept coming to mind.

Since I began the book, two significant developmentshave made me even more aware of the need to be ever mindful of the power and influence of network television news. During the latter part of 1994 and the early part of 1995, history was being made in the United States. For the first time in forty years, the Republicans took control of Congress in November of 1994. Another first for the country was when the Republican candidates adopted a "Contract with America," a program of what they would do if they were given control of Congress in the election. This, so far as I know, was the first time in history that Congressional candidates had run on a national program. This "Contract with America" called for certain very specific actions being taken, and when the new Congress convened in January of 1995, the Republicans in the House of Representatives immediately started trying to carry out the commitments of the Contract.

As I understand it, the main thrust of the Republicans' "Contract with America" is to reduce the size of the federal government in Washington, D. C., reduce the control of the federal government over the lives of the American people, and transfer back to the people and to the local and state governments the power that has gradually been brought to Washington over the past thirty or forty years. This action of returning power to the people and the local and state governments is simply the fulfillment of Article X of the Bill of Rights, which specifies that "The powers not delegated to the United States by the Constitution, nor prohibited by it to the States, are reserved to the States respectively, or to the people."

For reasons which I hope will become clear in the reading of this book, the networks have a vested interest in keeping power concentrated in Washington and are therefore likely to do everything they can to see to it that the Republicans and the "Contract with America" fail. For example, the network news reports continuously state that the Republicans' proposed tax bill "reduces" Medicare, something which will naturally be of concern to millions of Americans. That is a completely misleading statement, and the news media surely knows that it is misleading. Medicare is not reduced in the Republican plan; it will simply not increase at as large a percentage as proposed by the Democratic plan. The networks have consistently supported the liberal Democratic viewpoint and will, I believe, do all they can to help return liberal Democrats to power in the United States Congress as well as keep them in the White House.

The second significant development, perhaps the saddest in our recent history, was the bombing of the Alfred P. Murrah Federal Building in Oklahoma City on April 19, 1995. This was a terrible senseless tragedy; it should never have happened. Although some are now wanting to blame the tragedy on the rhetoric of "talk radio," it is just as conceivable that this senseless act was encouraged by the fact that over the last thirty years the national network news has emphasized controversy, generally by opposing the government, and has taken what the news media has referred to as an "adversarial" position to the government. The media has said that this is the proper position for them to take.

The way in which the national media, and particularly television, has reported on the Oklahoma City bombing also reflects the liberal point of view. As I watched the coverage, it reminded me of the coverage of the assassination of President John F. Kennedy in Dallas, Texas in 1963. Network news reports constantly blamed the assassination of Kennedy on the "conservative atmosphere in Dallas," although this had nothing whatever to do with the assassination itself. Since Kennedy was a very popular president, this constant "laying of the blame" at the door of the conservatives probably resulted in a substantial loss of respect among the American people for the conservative viewpoint. As a contrast, when the assassination attempt was made on President Ronald Reagan in 1981, there was never any attempt to blame it on the "liberal atmosphere in Washington, D. C."

There is now a very strong tendency on the part of the national news media to blame the Oklahoma City bombing on the far-right conservative viewpoints of a growing number of American people and on their talk about what they think the government should or should not do. I cannot help but wonder if this is an attempt to repeat what they did in 1963 so as to adversely affect people's respect for the conservative viewpoint and therefore possibly increase the chances of the liberal Democrats to regain power in 1996.

I did not have this view of the intentions of the networks when I first became involved with them in the late 1960s. Although I did believe that news reports were having a detrimental effect on the social and moral climate in our country, I believed it was possible that no one, including the networks themselves, was aware of the influence of these reports. As I pointed out earlier, at that time the news programs were erased after two weeks and there was no way for anyone to go back and see how a particular issue—for example, civil rights—had been covered. My current views are a result of eighteen years of experiences dealing with the networks, as well as experiences I had in Washington, D. C., New York, and throughout the country on business for the Archive and a lifetime of studying the network evening news as a concerned viewer.

This version of the history of the Vanderbilt Television News Archive is thus interwoven with my reflections and opinions about the impact of network television news on our country. All footnotes contained in the original documents appearing in the book were added at the time the book was written in 1994–95 and were not a part of the original documents. In a final chapter, I present some of my conclusions about what has taken place in this country since the founding of the Archive in August of 1968, and I try to give some guidelines on how to be a discerning viewer. It is my hope that readers will themselves develop a more skeptical attitude toward what they see and hear on network television news and that they will never forget what Fred Friendly and Ed Murrow recognized as the key to a successful television news program—"conviction, controversy, and a point of view."

Chapter One

Our History Lost:

The Importance of Preserving Television News

I think it was in 1967 that I saw Timothy Leary recommend on television news that young people learn who they were by freeing their minds by taking LSD. I could hardly believe this recommendation had been broadcast to millions of young people over national television. I wished I could see the program again to confirm exactly what had been said.

I had recently begun to be concerned about the impact of television news on our country, and this example in particular disturbed me. It is only one of many examples, but I must rely solely on memory for these recollections as there is no systematic way to check the record of what, when, or where something was broadcast on the nightly network news prior to August 5, 1968.

My concern about the effect television news was having on our country, combined with the fact that I have always been something of a "news buff," led me to become very interested in seeing how news programs were compiled. So when I knew at the end of 1967 that I would be going to New York (as I did several times a year in my job as a District Manager for Metropolitan Life Insurance Company), I contacted the networks to ask for permission to visit their news departments. Thus began a journey which consumed much of my time and energy for a period of more than eighteen years and by now has almost constantly occupied my mind for nearly thirty years.

I contacted the three television networks—ABC, CBS, and NBC—and told them I was very interested in how national television news programs were "put together." All three networks graciously responded to my request for a visit while I was in New York on March 25–27.

It was during these sessions in the news departments that I learned, to my surprise, that the nightly news broadcasts, a principal information source for America, were kept for only two weeks. The networks then erased the tapes and reused them. In a way, I understood the networks' position on this matter, for the two-inch tapes were bulky and expensive, and, after all, they were in the news business, not the library business. Yet this was a situation that I felt had to be corrected.

Right after my sessions at the networks I attended a speech given by John J. McCloy, a prominent New York attorney and banker who had also been High Commissioner to Germany after World War II. McCloy was also a board member of Metropolitan Life and past president of the Ford Foundation. I spoke with him briefly after the meeting about what I had just learned—the fact that the tapes were being erased. I asked for permission to call and talk with him. I did call him and he was interested enough in the issue of preserving television news to suggest that I contact Fred Friendly, the distinguished former CBS News president who was teaching journalism at Columbia University and was also the television advisor to the Ford Foundation. Mr. Friendly was not available, so I did not get to talk with him at that time.

To determine if the news was being archived anywhere, I called all over the country. I discovered that an Oregon university had some CBS material, but it turned out to be audiotapes primarily of CBS's radio news broadcasts from London during World War II. I heard that the Department of Defense had taped network news programs during the Vietnam War. I called a Defense Department representative and learned that they did tape the full network news and sent the compiled excerpts on the Vietnam War to the commanders in Vietnam so that they could see and hear what the American people were seeing and hearing about the war. (I suggested that they keep these tapes on a permanent basis and hoped they would index and abstract them some day so that scholars and historians could study them. I think these tapes are being retained. I hope so.) I also inquired at the Federal Communications Commission and at the Library of Congress. After my research I concluded that nowhere was the national network news being preserved in a systematic way.

First, I thought to establish a non-profit corporation to archive the news. I called Fred Friendly to talk about possible funding. He was out and so I talked to Richard Catalano, a Ford Foundation official. Based on our conversation, I felt it was highly unlikely that I would secure financial assistance from the foundation at that time for such an organization.

After thinking about it further, I thought that the news should be kept in a library, preferably a college library, just as newspapers and magazines have been kept for years. I considered that a university library would be a practical place to house a television news archive because it would be good for college students to have the material available, for I hoped that they would study it.

Having graduated from Vanderbilt University Law School and living in Nashville, Tennessee, I first thought of the Joint University Libraries that served Vanderbilt, Peabody, and Scarritt. In early June, I talked with Frank Grisham, associate director of the Joint University Libraries. He was interested and supportive and suggested that I prepare some material to present to a committee to be appointed by Chancellor Alexander Heard, who became interested in the project. I wrote the following document for that purpose:

OBSERVATIONS REGARDING
THE PRESERVATION OF
NATIONAL TELEVISION NEWS PROGRAMS

June 6, 1968

For a number of years I have been interested in national television news programs believing that they have a tremendous impact on events in the United States. Television news in effect presents the equivalent of a newspaper headline and lead paragraph concerning a limited number of national news items. Coverage in depth is possible only through documentaries run at intervals. A recent article in *Newsweek* magazine stated that 90% of the families earning $5,000 or less a year own television sets, which I am sure are watched extensively. In my opinion a very large number of these people do not read newspapers, magazines or books. Their entire knowledge of news therefore is based on what they see on television news programs. There are a very large number of other people who do have newspapers, magazines and books available to them but because of the pressure of time or other reasons depend on national television news programs for most of their information about news events other than those in their own community.

There are three major national television news programs—NBC Huntley Brinkley, CBS Cronkite and ABC Reynolds. In a great many areas either two or three of these programs come on the air at the same time. In

Nashville, for example, all three programs are scheduled for the same time. This really means that only one national television news program is available to the people in Nashville.

Because of the tremendous impact of television news programs, I wrote the television networks and asked to visit with them on a recent trip to New York. I spent about one and one-half hours each with the news departments of CBS, ABC and NBC. The men with whom I talked were most considerate and gave me full information as to how national news programs are "put together" for television. Briefly, the method consists of having assignment desks which assign camera crews to cover certain news events. These may be national network crews or may be crews from locally affiliated television stations. The national assignment desks make the assignments on the basis of what they and the program director consider to be the newsworthy events to occur that day. Local television affiliates may also call the assignment desk and report newsworthy items taking place in their area. They then may or may not be asked to cover these items and submit the film to the national network.

I gathered from my conversation with the networks that, on almost any given day, enough film and tape is available for the 30 minute program (commercials will take part of this 30 minutes) to provide at least one and one-half to three hours of program. It then becomes the responsibility of the Program Director and/or the Executive Producer to decide what part of the film and tape will be used. At the present time the impact of the news shown on the course of events is not subject to objective review as no copy of the actually taped program is retained on a permanent basis. The tape is kept for only a short time and then is erased and the tape reused. I am told that a copy of the script is kept at least for a year or two and that an effort is made to keep the film which is used. However, the film may be cut up and used in a documentary on the same subject at a later date. The result is that it would be extremely difficult, if not impossible, to recreate all the film used on a news program. It would be impossible to actually play back the program itself as it appeared.

Television news programs have had and are having such a tremendous impact on affairs in the United States it is difficult for me to understand how historians and scholars can review the course of events in the United States without having these actual programs readily available for review. Our libraries have files of books, magazines and newspapers available for review and study. It seems to me to be imperative that such libraries have files of television news network programs (exact recording) for review and study in the present and in the future. As technology for recording and storage improve, all television programs should be kept. At the present time it seems to me that it is most important to start with the national television news programs.

I have talked with the FCC and Library of Congress in Washington and with other sources including the television networks. So far as I am able to determine actual taped recordings of news programs are not kept and are not available anywhere. I have investigated enough to know that the expense of recording the three major television news network programs would not be great. The need appears to me to be exceptionally great.

Technical advances in tape recording and play-back and storage are being made constantly. For example I understand that CBS has an EVR system being developed which would make it possible to have one hour of video tape (black and white) transferred to film in a seven inch diameter and one-half inch thick cartridge. This cartridge could be placed in a play-back unit attached to a television set and played through the set with ability to stop and review any frame desired. The cost of the cartridge and play-back unit will be moderate. This system, or a similar system when perfected and introduced in 1969 or 1970, would make it possible for all major college libraries to have a file of the cartridges covering all television news network programs.[1]

The complete news programs once taped (and retained intact) could then be subdivided by subject matter and transferred to other tape or film which would include all television news network programming on a certain subject during a certain period of time. For example all CBS television news network program material on Vietnam during June, July and August 1968 could probably be included on one cartridge. Other subjects such as crime, civil rights and Election 1968 could be on other separate cartridges. It would then be very easy for a historian or scholar to place the cartridge in a play-back unit on a television set in a room in the library and review and study this film.

---

[1] I was fortunate enough to be asked by the local owner of a television station to fly with him on his plane to New York to see a demonstration of the system they wanted to develop. Because of what was said by CBS at that time, I was convinced that they would continue to develop this system and make it available. For some reasons unknown to me, the project was evidently discarded. (Author's comment, 1995)

I am completely sure that within two years at the most it will be relatively inexpensive for every major college library in the United States to have a television library to go with its present book, magazine and newspaper library.

In order for this to become an actuality, however, recordings must be made of present television news network programs NOW. As stated before, such recordings are not now available. Once shown on television and not recorded they are soon gone forever.

I do not believe that we would like to see newspapers published today distributed to the American people, read by them and then destroyed in their entirety so that days, months or years after they could not be reviewed. To make it even more comparable we could consider that only three newspapers reporting on national news events are published in the United States (all from New York); that because of limited space only headlines and a lead paragraph can be published on a limited number of news events; that these three national newspapers are destroyed in their entirety shortly after printing and distribution to the public and are, therefore, not ever afterward available for study or review by historians and scholars. We believe that this is in effect what is happening to television news programs today.

I do not see how historians and scholars could properly study the events of the last few years without being able to study the media which has probably had the biggest impact on the most people—national television news programs. I believe such "destruction" can and should be stopped by actually recording for future study, and that it should be stopped at the earliest possible moment. I believe that such recording can and should be done under the direction and control of a nationally recognized library without political or governmental control so that there could be no possible question of political or government censorship.

* * *

By late June, as I became more and more absorbed with this situation and more determined to try to do something about it, I felt it appropriate and necessary to contact my superiors at Metropolitan Life. On June 28, I wrote a letter informing them and acknowledging that "while it is completely clear that my position with Metropolitan has nothing to do with my interest and concern in this matter, it would be well for you to know of my activity." Knowing that my first priority would be to continue to perform satisfactorily for the company, Metropolitan Life officials permitted me the time to pursue this agenda.

Therefore, I continued my efforts to secure funding. I wrote the following observations in July, 1968, to distribute to people I thought might be interested in helping to fund the Archive.

OBSERVATIONS CONCERNING
NATIONAL TELEVISION NETWORK
NEWS PROGRAMS

July 17, 1968

There are apparently more and more people in the United States who are questioning the objectivity and impact of national television news programs. This is becoming a question of such importance that a thorough study seems to be needed.

Before such a study can be successfully conducted, it is necessary to understand how national television news programs are "put together". On a recent visit with the News Departments of CBS, ABC and NBC, I was given this information concerning the method of procedure for the news programs. Briefly, the method consists of having assignment desks which assign camera crews to cover certain news events. These may be national network crews or may be crews from locally affiliated television stations. The national assignment desks make the assignments on the basis of what they and the program director consider to be the most newsworthy events to occur that day. Local television affiliates may also call the assignment desk and report newsworthy items taking place in their area. They then may or may not be asked to cover these items and submit the film to the national network.

I gather from my conversations with the networks that, on almost any given day, enough film and tape of important usable news is available for the 30 minute program (commercials will take part of this 30 minutes) to provide at least one and one-half to three hours of program. It then becomes the responsibility of the Program Director and/or the Executive Producer to decide what part of the film or tape will be used. The responsibility and opportunity for the Program Director and/or the Executive Producer to decide which 20 minutes (approximately) of the 90 to 180 minutes of news available is to be shown to the American public is an awesome one. In effect, this decision is made by three men (one in each network), all three of whom live in New York and are subject to a "liberal" atmosphere which is frequently different from that of much of the United States. Each of these men must make a decision on how the news is presented and what news is presented. This decision has to be affected by his beliefs, his background and his surroundings no matter how hard he tries to maintain objectivity. If he is going to parties with friends who have certain beliefs, it is going to be difficult for him not to have these beliefs also and difficult for him to present something in a way that would cause his friends to berate him for having done so. Various sections of the United States have different sets of moral values and sets of "rights and wrongs." I do not believe that the "liberal" group in certain parts of the country would like to have the "conservative" morals of the Midwest or South featured in television news. Because all three network television news programs are controlled by men in the "liberal" atmosphere, this has caused confusion and anger in many parts of the country. The young people of our nation are confused and upset because their families and communities have reared them to believe in a certain set of morals and values and then on television they see an entirely different set. This is not to try to decide which set is right. It is just to say that for the first time in our history, a set of morals and values for the whole country is originating from a few people in one "liberal" atmosphere.

The real danger in our national television news programs is the fact that there are only three such programs, and these are controlled, in effect, by three individuals all living in the same area and atmosphere. It is made even more dangerous by the fact that the actual programs are not kept and reviewed so that even the person controlling the program may not be fully conscious of the cumulative impact of the manner in which he is presenting the news.

On my visit with the television News Departments, all three networks vigorously denied any control or bias in the news. I am convinced that all three of the people with whom I talked were honest in making this statement. However, I am also convinced that no one, including the head of each of the networks' News Department, really knows whether or not there is any bias and if so in what direction. I believe that there is only one way that an accurate appraisal can be made as to the objectivity of the news programs. This way is to permanently record the actual news programs themselves. The tape of the actual recording should be kept as a permanent record. I would then suggest that the programs be sub-divided into several particular news items such as Vietnam, crime, civil rights, Election 68 and so forth. All of the news on each program of these particular subjects should be on a separate tape. For example, one tape could contain all of NBC Huntley-Brinkley on Vietnam for a three or four month period of time. This would include possibly a minute from a program one day, a minute and one-half from the next day, two minutes from the following day and so forth. By playing this tape and studying it, it would then be possible for those in control of the national network news departments, as well as scholars and historians, to determine the impact of the news and also the objectivity of the news shown.

I note that in the article "Television Comes Under Fire" in the *U.S. News and World Report* of July 15, 1968 the following appears: "Nicholas Johnson, a member of the FCC, after an extensive study of the corporate structure of the television industry, says the power of this medium may be greater than that of the federal, State and local government all put together." Since the power of this medium is so great, the networks have a very strong responsibility to see that this power is properly exercised.

For the benefit of all concerned there is a real need for an objective review as to how this power is used. One man who often speaks for the administration on matters of national policy is quoted in the same article in *U.S. News and World Report* as saying "Even a raised eyebrow, or the inflection of a voice, or a caustic remark dropped into the middle of a news broadcast can create doubt. One television performer discussed the necessary delays by the State Department in setting up peace talks with North Vietnam. Then he dropped the remark: 'It appears that the Administration does not want to negotiate as much as it says it does.'"

The only way that the impact of a "raised eyebrow or the inflection of a voice" can actually be studied is through recording so that it is possible to determine whether or not the "raised eyebrow or the inflection of a voice" is accidental or by design. Once could be accidental. Repetition would tend to indicate design.

I believe the national networks should be pleased to have historians and scholars review the news programs in studying the history of events in the United States and in studying the impact and objectivity of the programs. The question of impact and objectivity could then be finally resolved.

If too many people lose their confidence in the objectivity of news programs, the networks will lose income from sponsors as the listening audience will decrease.

There is a growing need for a return of full confidence in the national television network news programs. This full confidence can be restored only by definite proof (through recording and study) that the news programs are fairly and objectively "put together".

On July 29, Chancellor Alexander Heard appointed the ad hoc University committee to move the project forward and to develop a feasibility proposal. The first Vanderbilt faculty and staff to be formally involved were the following:

- Mr. Robert A. McGaw (Secretary of Vanderbilt University)
- Professor Paul Bergeron (History)
- Dean Emmett Fields (Dean of the College of Arts & Sciences)
- Mr. Frank Grisham (Associate Director of Joint University Libraries)
- Professor Paul Hardacre (History)
- Professor Leiper Freeman (Political Science)

I met with the committee right away. They were interested in my ideas about preserving the news on video tape. We debated eliminating commercials during broadcasts to save money but then decided only two programs would fit on a one-hour tape anyway. I thought we should start the recorder when the program began and stop it when the program ended. That way everything would be recorded just as it was broadcast, without any breaks.

From the beginning, I was concerned not only with preserving the original broadcast completely intact for reference but also compiling subject tapes, for I felt that was the only way that television news would be studied by scholars as well as by the producers and directors at the networks. I was looking for the appropriate equipment and procedures that would keep the original tapes untouched and yet permit the production of subject tapes. I felt it was critical that the original tapes be retained in their entirety so that anyone who wished to see them could do so.

I talked to Jack DeWitt, a Nashville pioneer in radio and television about what tapes and equipment to use. He recommended one-inch black-

and-white Ampex reel-to-reel equipment. I then flew to Chicago (at my own expense) and spent a day talking with the people at the Ampex Corporation. They were very much interested in the entire matter and indicated that Ampex would be interested in helping in some fashion with equipment and tape. They also assured me that equipment existed to enable the production of subject matter tapes while leaving the original master intact.

After I returned from Chicago, I met with the Vanderbilt committee. Suddenly the thought occurred to us that the election of 1968 would make a good experimental project to show that taping on a regular basis could be done. We thought this project would be a good feasibility study and also serve a useful purpose.

Vanderbilt University approved the idea. Arrangements were made with the local Ampex dealer, Nicholson's Stereo. The dealer agreed to furnish three video tape recording machines and to install them in the rare book room at the library so that we could secure them at night. Ron Moulton, who was working for Nicholson's, set up the equipment and showed me how to use it. Ampex Corporation furnished ten rolls of video tape. In return for the loan of the equipment, we agreed to purchase the rest of the tape stock at retail rather than wholesale prices. I made a contribution to Vanderbilt University of a sufficient amount to cover the cost of the remaining tape needed: $3,922. Fortunately, costs were less in 1968 so that I did not have to put up the equivalent $16,000 or more that would be required today.

Because the Republicans were the party out of power, the Republican Convention met first beginning on August 5, 1968. That night I began taping the nightly news from all three networks and then taped the convention itself. We had only three reel-to-reel machines. I couldn't take the time to rewind the tapes because too much of the program would be missed. I just removed one reel and replaced it as quickly as I could. Late at night after the convention ended, sometimes as late as two or three in the morning, I rewound the tapes. The Democratic Convention was in September. I taped both conventions and the nightly news on all three networks. Frank Grisham helped me do some of the recording.

Our major project was to record the three evening news programs to prove it could be done. We felt that they were the major news programming in the country and the most likely to be continued. We intended to record the conventions since we were planning on making the three-month project cover the 1968 national election—beginning with the first convention and ending the day after the election in November. Our plan was to record the news off the air just as it was broadcast in Nashville, and our intentions always were to erase the convention coverage and reuse the tapes for the daily news programs if that became financially necessary.

We continued to record the evening newscasts and transferred the equipment to another small room in the library. Before long we were able to get students to help with the ongoing taping.

My original money began to run out, yet I did not want to erase the national convention coverage if we could help it. I approached a Nashville businessman and friend, Jack C. Massey, explaining that if we did not receive additional funding, we would have to erase convention coverage. Because of the violence in Chicago at the Democratic Convention in September and the great publicity given to that event, neither he nor I wanted to erase the convention coverage. Consequently, Jack Massey donated $7,500 to the Archive. I also went to David K. (Pat) Wilson, whom I knew, and asked for his assistance. He also donated $7,500. Mr. Massey's and Mr. Wilson's support was absolutely critical to the Archive's ability to operate. In September, the Vanderbilt Board of Trust contributed $5,540 in cash. During this meeting Chancellor Heard indicated his belief in and strong support of the project.

These funds enabled us to continue. Later in September, Chancellor Heard and I were by coincidence in New York on the same day. He suggested that we talk to Fred Friendly about the project and possible assistance from the Ford Foundation. Heard found that Friendly would not be available that day and Heard had to return to Nashville that evening. Since he could not stay over and see Friendly the next day as I could, he dictated a letter asking for the Foundation's financial assistance to continue the project. At Heard's request, I signed the transcribed letter for him and delivered it the next day when I met with Friendly at Columbia University. Friendly was interested, but he thought that, for various reasons, there should be a feasibility study by professionals in the field. We had a very positive conversation, but I think he and I both felt that he would probably not recommend financial help at that time from the

Ford Foundation. He said with a laugh, "It will probably take someone like you who doesn't know any better to get it done."

I was determined to see this done, for I believed that it was extremely important for copies of the original news programs to be available for study. I also believed it was important to prepare from the original programs compiled subject matter tapes on subjects such as Vietnam, crime and violence, etc. I felt that this procedure would make the Archive genuinely useful. It was my hope that eventually libraries throughout the United States would have television news libraries with at least copies of the subject matter tapes so that the impact of television coverage in the United States could be studied by as many people as possible.

Very soon there was an occasion to prepare the first subject matter tape. Although we made no effort to hide what we were doing, not many people knew about us in 1968. However, the Ampex Corporation did. They requested that a tape on the violence in the streets during the Chicago convention be prepared for their use at the International Police Convention in Hawaii in October. I was happy to comply with their request to satisfy myself that it was possible to produce a compiled tape on a single subject and leave the master tape completely intact. We selected the NBC coverage to examine solely on the basis that NBC had the best ratings at the time and so arguably had the greatest impact because it was seen by the greatest number of people.

I sat down and looked through NBC's coverage of the Democratic Convention and made what amounted to an abstract. I listed the items involving violence and the items involving comments from the convention and the convention floor about the violence. After Nicholson's let us borrow a machine that could edit tape segments together, Ron Moulton and I made the compiled tape. As we were doing this, I saw the same heavy man with a plaid shirt and a beard being arrested and put in the paddy wagon three times. That's when I came to realize that it was the same scene of violence taped from three different angles.

Anti-Vietnam demonstrations had been previously rumored and promised for Chicago's convention. When the networks set up lights to record the night's activity, protestors were drawn to the lighted location. The networks knew that the protestors were going to come and they did; therefore, they set up three different cameras at the corner of Balboa and Michigan Streets. NBC taped the action and ran the footage from two cameras while the convention was in progress. Then an hour later NBC said, "We will now show you the latest violence at 501 Michigan Street," and they showed the footage from the third camera, but it was the same big man in the plaid shirt going into the paddy wagon again. In effect, their coverage depicted ongoing violence, but they were showing the same previously videotaped scene. I don't think they were deliberately trying to distort reality. I understand they were unable to use live remote footage due to the telephone strike in Chicago, but the fact is that they did show the same footage more than once and in their commentary presented it as more than one occurrence. This technique gave a mistaken impression of the nature of the violence during the convention.

This incident can be substantiated because in Theodore White's book, *The Making of the President 1968*, White wrote that he was in Hubert Humphrey's hotel room on September 28. When Humphrey saw the televised violence, he inquired about the action out his window that overlooked the corner of Balboa and Michigan Streets. An aide told him that everything was dark and quiet down there. According to Theodore White, Humphrey said, "I'm going to be President someday. . . . I'm going to appoint the FCC—we're going to look into all this!" (p. 302) No doubt Humphrey was especially interested because NBC showed the demonstration footage (again) instead of showing the live convention floor coverage, where Humphrey's nomination for President was being seconded.

The October 7, 1968, issue of *Broadcasting*, a publication that the industry heavily relied on during that era, carried an article on page 52 entitled "Southern Eye Fixed on the Networks: Nashville businessmen back project to record and catalogue all network news." The article called national attention to our efforts as well as questioned whether the Archive "will benefit future historians or prove a noisome index of alleged bias in the way the networks report the news." Jack Massey was quoted in the article as saying he supported the project because "it is needed in this country—necessary, good information to have. Do you know that TV news media influence people more than newspapers? And when the three TV outfits (networks) can say things that are not fair or unbiased, then people ought to know about it."

We had demonstrated that it was possible to tape the news and other specialized news programming such as the conventions, that it was possible to compile a tape on one subject, and that studying the news in such a fashion might lead to some interesting, even critical, insights into this powerful cultural force. In October, I wrote a proposal in the name of Vanderbilt University to seek funds to operate the Archive for three years. We thought this amount of time would be reasonable to establish further the obvious value of the collection and to find a more suitable home, such as the Library of Congress, for the collection and the ongoing work of the taping. A copy of this proposal can be found in Appendix A.

By the end of 1968, I was more convinced than ever that we were on to something monumentally important and that I had to secure funds to continue. The Archive, moreover, seemed to have a life of its own. In the next year the project attracted the attention of the networks, as well as the White House.

Chapter Two

Conviction, Controversy, and a Point of View:

Are Network News Programs Objective?

I felt that it was very important to keep the networks informed about what we were doing at the Archive, and in addition the Archive could more easily reach its full potential if we had the support and assistance of the networks. Early in 1969, I wrote to each of the networks to let them know I would be coming back to New York on business and would like to meet with them to further explain the Vanderbilt project. George Jenkins, chairman of the Finance Committee for Metropolitan Life, was on the Board of Directors at ABC at that time, and he had arranged a meeting for me with Everett Erlick, group vice-president at ABC. I confirmed the meeting with Erlick in a letter which summarized the project and my interest in national television news programs; I sent him copies of the "Observations Regarding the Preservation of National Television News Programs," "Progress Report on a Proposed National

News Library," and "Proposal for Television News Library Project." I also sent the same letter and materials to Frank Stanton, president of CBS, and to Julian Goodman, president of NBC. I added a paragraph in the NBC letter explaining that we had made two subject matter tapes—one of material shown by NBC concerning violence during the Democratic Convention on August 28, 1968, and another one including everything on the subject of law and order shown on NBC from August 5-29, 1968. In my letter, I indicated that we would be happy for NBC to see these tapes.

My meeting with Erlick at ABC on January 29, 1969, was very cordial, and I felt that he had a much better understanding of what we were trying to do by the end of the meeting. In the course of our meeting, I raised the question of financial assistance. I pointed out that I knew that financing was going to be a problem, but that I was determined to keep the Archive going even if I had to get out on the street with a tin cup. Fortunately, things didn't get to that point. There was never any indication from Erlick that he felt our idea of taping national news programs was a bad idea, and no mention of our right (or the lack of such) to do what we were doing came up during our conversation. I noticed this fact particularly because in my meeting with CBS the previous day, CBS representatives had tentatively raised the question of whether we had a legal right to record its news programs.

My request for a meeting with CBS had been referred to Robert Evans, vice-president and general counsel, so I met with Evans and a member of the CBS legal staff for about an hour and a half. The general tone of this meeting was also cordial, and I felt that they too left the meeting with a much better understanding of what we were trying to accomplish. No one at the meeting ever stated that CBS would prefer that we not be recording news programs, but they did talk generally about what CBS might do regarding this material in the future should any question about the legality of what we were doing arise. I emphasized to all three networks that the only reason Vanderbilt was keeping these tapes was that they were not being kept by the networks and that if the networks would begin to keep the tapes and make them available to the public, I would do my best to persuade Vanderbilt to give the networks the tapes they had.

At NBC, I met with Thomas Ervin, executive vice-president, and two news department staff members. They also questioned whether or not we had a legal right to record NBC's news programs. Ervin stated that they were not going to tell us that we could tape and they were not going to tell us that we couldn't. I responded that we were not going to ask if we could. I felt that this position was best for NBC because if the network had agreed to let us tape the programs, it may have had some problems when officials started renewing contracts with news anchors or staff—they could have wanted to receive a fee for each copy of the program. The best arrangement all around was for Vanderbilt to be taping the news programs off the air as they were presented to the American people. I tried to make clear that our interest was in seeing that the material was kept and that we wanted the networks to understand what we were doing.

I had taken the two subject matter tapes with me and had them in my briefcase at my feet during this conversation. Twice, I mentioned that I had the tapes with me. The only question raised concerning the tapes was the length of the general violence tape, which was sixty minutes. The NBC representatives didn't ask to see the tapes, so I didn't make any further offers to show them. An interesting conversation had occurred when I met with Robert Evans at CBS the day before. He asked me if I knew that NBC had appointed a new executive producer of its evening news program. I couldn't understand why he went out of his way to make this comment. Thinking about it, I wondered if it had anything to do with that scene of violence being shown three different times from different angles, since the executive producer could have been the producer responsible for that representation. Perhaps NBC thought that by bringing the tapes with me, I was planning to publicize the fact that NBC had shown the same coverage three times.

I really had no interest in doing that. I wanted to work with the networks and went out of my way not to be too critical of them. At all three of these meetings, I requested financial assistance from the networks and copies of their news logs. At this point, Vanderbilt did not have the money to complete an index and abstracts. We had only enough money to tape the program, label the box with the date and the name of the network, and put it on a shelf. It was really not very usable because there was no easy way to find out what was on that particular program. We thought a copy of the logs from the networks would give us that information. Even though the archive wasn't very usable at this point, the reason we kept taping and putting tapes on the shelf was that unless we did, when we got the money to complete an index and abstracts, the original materials would not be available since tapes of the programs were not being kept elsewhere. I tried to make it clear that we were not wanting to attack the networks but were simply trying to make this material available for study. Though we felt that all the networks better understood what we were doing, none agreed to provide assistance at that time. Although we had not asked any of the networks for permission to tape their news programs, a follow-up letter from Robert Evans of CBS in March of 1969 pointed out that CBS would not grant us permission to record its broadcasts off the air.

I didn't believe we needed permission, but I *knew* that we needed financing. I continued talking with a number of people about how best to continue this important work. I called Robert MacNeil, author of the book *The People Machine.* MacNeil was in London at the time, and we talked at length about the project. He seemed to agree that the project was important and should be continued. He suggested that I contact Federal Communications Commissioner Nicholas Johnson, a friend of his who he believed would be very interested in the matter. He thought that the FCC might be able to suggest financing options for the Archive. After this conversation, I sent a letter and various materials to Commissioner Johnson and to each of the other FCC commissioners. Sending him various materials about the Archive, I also followed up with a letter to Robert MacNeil. Although I never heard anything further from him, my talk with MacNeil could not have come at a better time. I was in the midst of one of my, as I phrased it to him, "spells of discouragement." His interest in the project gave me renewed determination to make every effort to see that the Archive continued.

At that time, everyone involved with the Archive felt that the Library of Congress was the appropriate agency to take on the project. In preparation for an approach to the Library of Congress, I sent complete information about the Archive to Senators Albert Gore, Sr., and Howard Baker and to Congressmen Bill Brock and Richard Fulton. In early March of 1969, I went to Washington to talk with them directly about what we were doing. All of these men became interested in the project and wrote a joint letter to the librarian of Congress encouraging the Library of Congress to study the feasibility of assuming responsibility for continuing this work.

During this same trip to Washington, I also visited with several staff members at the Library of Congress. I contacted Donald Leavitt, head of the Recorded Sound Section, at the suggestion of Frank Grisham. Leavitt was very pleased to know that somebody somewhere was keeping tapes of the national network news. He was so pleased that he called a colleague in the Library of Congress to tell him about what we were doing. We discussed the archive project at some length, and Leavitt then introduced me to other staff members who he thought would be interested. After extensive discussion with various people and a definite expression of interest on their part, it was decided that I would suggest to the committee at Vanderbilt that they write a letter to L. Quincy Mumford, librarian of Congress, to outline what we had been doing and to ask him to look into the possibility of the Library of Congress' taking over the project. This letter was subsequently sent under Robert McGaw's signature, to explain our interest in the project, to outline what had been done to date, and to invite staff members to visit the Archive at Vanderbilt to see the project in operation. The Library of Congress did undertake a feasibility study, and on June 3, 1969, staff members Alan Fern, John Kuiper, and Donald Leavitt came to Nashville to see what we were doing.

Around the same time, the librarian of Congress also wrote to the president of each of the three networks about establishing a news archive as a project of the Library of Congress. ABC seemed rather interested in the idea and sent James Hagerty, vice-president, to Washington to talk to the librarian of Congress. NBC sent two members of its Washington office to talk about the idea. They told the librarian of Congress that he would hear from them after they talked with NBC's New York office. However, as far as I know, nothing further was heard from NBC. I was told that the CBS president never acknowledged the first letter from the librarian of Congress, nor to my knowledge did he ever acknowledge the follow-up letter that was mailed in the fall of 1969. This behavior was difficult for me to understand, as I felt that the librarian of Congress was an important enough person to at least have his letters acknowledged by the president of the CBS network.

In June, 1969, I had a bit of time on my hands, as well as an excellent secretary, so I wrote some "Observations" about our archive project based on my experience to date in hopes that the document would assist in my fund-raising efforts.

OBSERVATIONS CONCERNING NATIONAL NETWORK TELEVISION NEWS PROGRAMS

June 2, 1969

Having been much involved in recording on video tape the three daily national network television news programs since August 5, 1968 and having given a great deal of thought and consideration to the entire subject of national television news programs, I have come to the following conclusions.

It seems almost "horrible" to me that we are not keeping on a permanent basis information of great value to future historians and other scholars. Ten, fifteen, twenty or more years from now it would be invaluable to have for study the actual television network news programs. These would give a very comprehensive picture of life in the United States and the world. Historians and scholars are spending millions of dollars to try to gather or recover information on the past which is not nearly as valuable as the actual copies of the television news programs would be in the future. If the programs were actually going to be sealed and not even subject to review for 25 or 50 years, they should still be kept.

I am convinced, however, that these programs are of such tremendous impact currently that they need to be kept and made widely available for study as to the trend of their impact. I am sure that the people in overall control of the three national networks are making an effort to present the news as fairly as possible. Unfortunately, I have also come to the conclusion that the people in overall control of the networks are not completely conscious of the impact of the news being presented on their programs. I doubt that they have ever been able to sit down and review their news programs for a long period of time. I doubt that they have ever reviewed subject matter tapes showing how their network program has presented the news on a particular subject over a period of time. For example, I doubt that anyone in any of the networks has reviewed their network's news presentation of the college disorders for a period of six or seven months time. I am also sure that the people in overall charge of the networks are not the ones who make the decisions on a day to day basis as to what news is shown and how it is shown. I think that this is very clearly indicated in Fred Friendly's book, DUE TO CIRCUMSTANCES BEYOND OUR CONTROL [published by Random House in 1967], when he indicates on page 216 as follows: "On another occasion a projected half-hour interview with Senator William Fulbright conducted by Eric Sevareid and Martin Agronsky so upset Stanton that he said, 'What a dirty trick that was to play on the President of the United States — I didn't know about it until I saw the news release,'" and then again on page 217 as follows: "His objections to such broadcasts were, he told me, partly financial (though each of the Vietnam debates cost no more than $10,000), but were mainly based on his concern that too much "dove-hawk" talk unsteadies the hand of the Commander-in-Chief."

I believe that it is impossible for the people charged with the responsibility for the networks to properly carry out this responsibility without having subject matter tapes to review from time to time to determine that the news is being presented on an objective basis. Even if every effort is made to present the news objectively, the personal opinions of the person or persons making the actual day to day decisions as to what is shown on the news programs and how it is shown will have to have a major influence. Personal opinion must affect the decisions of the person who makes the decision as to what news is covered, how it is covered and what part of the several hours of tape and film available is shown to the American public each day. Deciding what is shown and how is a terrific responsibility which is not now subject to review by anyone on a continuous study basis.

I have come to the reluctant conclusion that it may be impossible for any Administration or any Congress to successfully govern the United States so long as we have our present situation in national television news coverage. Fred Friendly in the same book referred to above on page two reports as follows: "In the course of his introduction, Ed (Murrow) said to the television audience: 'This is an old team trying to learn a new trade.' It took us two years to learn that job. There was a one-hour report via television, but for the most part we were, as Ed said, just a bunch of old radio hands learning the hard way that cameras need something more than emulsion and light valves to create electronic journalism. The missing ingredients were conviction, controversy and a point of view."[1] We believe the key sentence in the above material is *"the missing ingredients were conviction, controversy and a point of view"*. We believe that Mr. Friendly is completely correct when he indicates that television news has endeavored to build and keep its audience of approximately 40 million people every week day by stressing "conviction, controversy and a point of view." Such action on the part of a profit making, audience seeking media may be necessary. It may be impossible for a network to operate a successful (in terms of advertising dollar received and viewing audience secured) news program without stressing "conviction, controversy and a point of view." This may be particularly true since in most major markets either two or three of the network news programs come on at the same time each day. Some reason must be developed to cause the viewer to select one network news program over the other one or two (he cannot see all three). Perhaps "controversy" is the key to success. Also perhaps this is one of the reasons controversy is tearing our country apart today.

The reason that we think it may be impossible for Congress or any Administration to govern the United States is that "controversy" can only be stirred up by opposing the people with the responsibility of operating the country. You do not have "controversy" by supporting the majority view or the view of those in

---

[1] The first "See It Now" television program was in December, 1951. Ed Murrow was at this point in time probably one of the most important and influential people in the news business. Fred Friendly later became president of CBS News. These two men undoubtedly influenced the trend the networks took in presenting the news. (Author's comment, 1995)

authority. "Controversy" is most frequently produced when you present the arguments and antics of the minority who are usually opposing those in authority. You certainly do not encourage calm reasoning progress by featuring "controversy."

We believe a thorough study of the daily network television news programs will reveal that those people, members of Congress and others, who have most frequently appeared on television news programs were those people who had recognized that the way to get "on television" was to furnish to the television networks the commodity they sought —"controversy."[2] Those members of Congress who are supporting an Administration (Democrat or Republican) and who are trying to proceed in an orderly and logical manner to carry out their responsibility are seldom seen on the television news. If they are seen it is infrequently and for a very short period of time.

It is important that any Administration or Congress have the opportunity to make decisions that are best for the country, keeping in mind at all times the desires and welfare of the American people. They should not *have* to make decisions to try to prevent a "controversial storm" on national television. Great study needs to be given to the question of whether or not national television reports opinion or makes opinion.

If the television networks decide to "push controversy" they apparently can "sell controversy" to the American public. Hard-headed American

---

[2] They are even more likely to be on television news if, in addition to "controversy," they speak from a "conviction" and "point of view" equivalent to that of the network news producer. (Author's comment, 1995)

businessmen are spending billions of dollars a year on television advertisement because they believe television can sell their product.

It is entirely possible to say that newspapers and magazines have stressed this same "controversy" over the years. There are several tremendous differences. First, no newspaper or magazine has an audience even approaching that of the television network news programs. Also, most of those people who would be influenced by a controversial newspaper or magazine article will also read newspapers or magazines presenting the other side. A very large number of those people watching a national network news program do *not* read newspapers or magazines to any extent. Also in most places in the United States the national network news programs come on the air at the same time. A person can watch only one of the programs and has no way to compare what he sees on this program with what he might have seen on another network program on the same day. He can, of course, read a newspaper or magazine today and then later in the day read another newspaper or magazine with a different presentation of the same subject.

The New York Times is certainly considered to be one of the most (if not the most) influential newspapers.[3]

---

[3] My study and experience led me to understand that the producers of each of the network news programs, when they met in the morning to decide on the news events in the nation and world to be covered that day, would give great importance to covering those stories on the front page of the *New York Times* and to a somewhat lesser degree on the front page of the *Washington Post*. I came to understand that we did have a "national news media" made up of the *New York Times*, the *Washington Post* (and occasionally the *Los Angeles Times*), and the three networks. The networks were, to some extent at least, the national voice of these newspapers. (Author's comment, 1995)

"Ayers" [a publication providing statistical information about national newspapers] shows in 1968 daily circulation of the *Times* as 840,495. I am sure that a very large percentage of these 840,495 readers also read at least one other daily newspaper and also read many magazines and books and watch television. Contrast 840,495 with 16,370,000 which is the number of television viewers estimated for the CBS Cronkite news program on Oct. 1, 1968 (a low period— it increases in the winter). Remember that a large number of these 16,370,000 cannot see the NBC Huntley-Brinkley or the ABC Reynolds news programs as they come on at the same time as the Cronkite program. Also remember that a very large number of these 16,370,000 do *not* read newspapers, magazines or books.

Every survey made indicates that more and more people are depending on television news programs for their news coverage. It also indicates that more and more people believe what they see on television as compared with what they read. We think this is clearly accounted for by the fact that people have a tendency to believe that what they see must be true. They do not stop to realize that they have been shown only what someone wanted them to see or decided what they should see.[4] Also because of the fact that the national

---

[4] Most people do not realize that what is shown on television news is a result of the "conviction" and "point of view" of the producer of the program. The cameraman is directed to take pictures which will help in presenting this. For example, if there is a small crowd but the producer wishes it to appear to be large, the cameraman will take a closeup shot showing only people, no vacant spaces. If, on the other hand, there is a large crowd but the producer wishes it to appear small, the cameraman will move his camera back to show vacant spaces, thus giving the impression of a small crowd. There are a great many other possible ways to use the camera to present a particular point of view. Some people seem to think that a camera takes pictures by itself. They don't stop to realize that someone has to point the camera where he wants it and take the picture he wants to take. (Author's comment, 1995)

network television news programs come on at the same time, they have nothing with which to compare a program. They can read a morning newspaper presenting news from one side and an evening newspaper presenting the same news from another side and realize that there are different ways of presenting things.[5] When they see a television news program presented from only one side they have no way of comparing how it might be presented from a different side.

Every major business concern in the United States has one or more publications. These newspapers or magazines are used by this business concern to communicate with its employees and stockholders and in many cases with its customers. I am sure that business concerns would be "horrified" at the idea of turning the publication of these newspapers and magazines over to someone other than the company to publish. I certainly do not believe that they would want these publications to be printed primarily to feature "controversy." I do not believe that many major business concerns could long successfully operate if someone was publishing their newspapers and magazines to feature "controversy" and criticism of the company's actions. I am sure that every company does make decisions and does have actions which at least someone would oppose. The company publications certainly do not give that person who

---

[5]   Each paper, morning and evening, may receive the same material on the wires from the Associated Press, but each newspaper will run in its paper only the parts it wishes to run and may even occasionally do some rewriting. The local television station, on the other hand, is simply a "conduit" for the national news programs and has no control over content. (Author's comment, 1995)

opposes (often without carefully considering why he opposes or knowing the reasons for the company action) the right to take over the newspaper or magazine and publish it.

The National Administration and Congress are entirely subject to the decision makers on the national network television news programs as to how their actions and decisions are communicated to the "employees, stockholders and customers" of the National Administration and Congress—the American public.

The Administration and Congress are faced with the terrible responsibility of governing the United States. They do not have the opportunity so far as the major communications media is concerned (television) to communicate with the American people which all corporations have in communicating with *their* employees, stockholders and customers.

In every major business or social (school or church) organization that exists the people charged with the responsibility for the successful operation of this business or social organization are given control of their media of communications with their "employees, stockholders or customers." This is definitely not true of the Congress or the Administration. The question of whether it should be true of Congress and the Administration is certainly subject to question. However, the conditions created by this lack of control deserve thorough study and consideration.

The people charged with the responsibility for our great country have no control over the television news media. The people who control the television news media have no responsibility for the country.

In January 1969 Congress devoted a great deal of study, and the news media a great deal of space, to the question of confirming executive appointments. Certainly this deserved to be done. However, at the same time a new Executive Producer of one of the television network news shows was appointed. This appointment of a man whose decisions could very strongly affect the country was not studied by Congress and received almost no notice by the news media.[6]

I am completely aware that the conclusions which I have reached have not been based on a thorough comprehensive study of the national network television news programs. While we have recorded these daily programs since August 5, 1968, we have not had the necessary funds to have the programs indexed and to have subject matter tapes developed (we have completed only two subject matter tapes to prove this could be done). At the present time in my opinion there is no way that anyone inside or outside of the networks can truthfully say that "this is the impact of the news programs shown." This will never be able to be done until someone in addition to keeping the daily television network news programs also indexes these programs and then develops subject matter tapes. The extreme importance of subject matter tapes is in my opinion that it is impossible for many people to sit down even with a comprehensive index and look through two or three months of the Cronkite news program and examine how a particular subject, Vietnam, student disorders, or any

---

[6] The executive producer of the evening news programs, with his ability to determine what the American people see and therefore believe, in the opinion of many people, has more actual power and impact than any member of the cabinet, even the Secretary of State or Defense. (Author's comment, 1995)

other subject has been covered over a period of two or three months' time. Most subjects covered by a national network television news program on a given day are covered in a manner equivalent to a newspaper headline and lead paragraph. In many cases the time devoted on a given day to a particular subject will run from 30 seconds to a maximum of a few minutes. The only way in my opinion for a large number of scholars to study the impact of the television news programs is to be able to see on one tape the material shown over a period of a month's time on a given subject.

I feel very strongly that the impact of newspapers and magazines on the American public as compared with the impact of the national television network news programs is the same as a comparison of the impact of the World War II conventional bomb with that of an atomic or hydrogen bomb. Controversy in newspapers and magazines may, like conventional bombs, be something we can survive. Controversy in television may be like atom or hydrogen bombs— something we cannot survive. [7]

Certainly the successful survival of the United States is so important that anything which drastically affects such survival deserves to be studied. Television news programs can only be studied properly and widely (as they deserve) if actual copies of the programs are kept and made as widely available as possible. Such study

---

[7] If this "controversy" is stirred up to promote "conviction" and a "point of view" different from that of the government or the American people, it becomes even more damaging to our survival. (Author's comment, 1995)

would also be made widely possible by preparing subject matter tapes (if anyone questioned the truth or completeness of the subject matter tapes they could always examine the original complete tapes from which the subject matter tape was prepared). [8]

※

As I said, in talking with the senators and congressmen in March, I had mentioned the compiled tape of the Democratic Convention violence I'd made at the end of 1968. I thought they might like for their staff to see the tape, so I mentioned the possibility of bringing the tape to Washington and showing it to them and their staff. Lee Smith, Senator Howard Baker's legislative assistant, made arrangements to show the tape and told me that we were going to show it in the Executive Office Building. I thought about this suggestion; then I called back because I really didn't think the White House ought to be involved. My feeling at that point was that the President of the United States had to be interested in network news because it was primarily about the President. Every evening news program starts with what the President and Congress have done, particularly the President, so he has to be interested. However, I didn't think the White House ought to become involved in any controversy with the networks. When I called Lee back, he repeated that they wanted to show the tape in the

---

8 The "outtakes" for these compiled tapes would always be preserved and available for review by anyone, unlike the outtakes of the networks from which their evening news has been excerpted. Through the years, the networks have steadfastly refused to permit these outtakes to be seen by anyone, even Congress. For example, during the Westmoreland hearings, Congress was unable to get outtakes, even though by refusing, the networks risked a contempt of Congress citation. (Author's comment, 1995)

Executive Office Building, so I said okay. In early October, 1969, I took the tape to the top floor of the Executive Office Building (adjoining the White House and housing offices of many members of the Executive Branch, including the President) where they had set up a closed circuit television which went to every office in the White House and the Executive Office Building. I pointed out that I was not going to show the full hour of the tape that we completed. I was just going to show parts of it. Then I went down to an EOB office where there were nine men waiting to watch the tape, including representatives from the offices of Senator Baker, Congressman Brock, and Congressman Fulton; three Nixon administration executive staff members; the co-director of the Media Task Force of the Eisenhower Commission on the Causes and Prevention of Violence; and the minority counsel of the Senate Commerce Committee.

After the showing, I returned to Nashville with the tape. Soon afterward, I came back from lunch one day, and my secretary said that Patrick Buchanan in the White House had been trying to reach me. I returned the call, and he asked if I would bring the tape back so that he could look at it. That's when I realized why it was shown in the first place from the closed circuit television in the Executive Office Building. Patrick Buchanan wasn't the only one who viewed it; there were others who had looked at it, too. Now this is just my guess—I never asked Lee Smith about it—but I think they wanted to look at it by themselves in their own offices rather than attending this meeting with the other representatives. The only way they could do that was to have it shown on the closed circuit basis. Perhaps they didn't have time to come to the meeting, and Pat Buchanan probably wasn't sure at that time if he wanted to be involved. He wanted to watch in the privacy of his own office before he made that decision.

Anyway, when I talked with Pat Buchanan on the phone, he offered to pay my expenses to bring the tape back to Washington. I told him I'd bring the tape back, but that I'd pay my own expenses. Before I made the trip, I sent Buchanan a letter confirming this arrangement, along with a substantial amount of material about the Archive, including a document entitled "Memorandum for National Administration." I had prepared this memorandum in January but had never submitted it to anyone for fear that it would be misunderstood as an effort by me to secure a job with the administration. I pointed out in my letter to Buchanan that this certainly was not the case and that I was sending him the memorandum because of his interest in and knowledge about television news.

Memorandum for National Administration

Jan. 31, 1969

I noticed recently in the newspapers that President Nixon reads the *New York Times* and the *Washington Post* each morning as he is having breakfast. I know that these two newspapers are extremely important in affecting and reflecting the thoughts and opinions of the "decision makers" in the United States. It is certainly important that the President of the United States has this information.

Having spent a very great deal of time during the past year in studying and recording the national network television news programs, I believe that these programs are having a tremendous impact on the country. Enclosed is material outlining what has been done and what we hope to do. Included in this material is a copy of a letter sent to each Federal Communications Commissioner.

I believe that it is vitally important that the National Administration, which represents all of us in the United States, know what the "decision makers" are thinking and what is affecting their thoughts, but I also believe that it is vitally important that our National Administration be constantly aware of what the great bulk of the American people are thinking and what they will think. The three national network television news programs reach from 37 million to 47 million homes every weekday night (number varying by season of the year). The total daily circulation of all evening newspapers in the United States (1,463 newspapers) in 1968 was 35,862,987.

I believe that it is imperative for the welfare of the country that the National Administration be constantly aware of the trend of thinking that is being developed among the American people by that which is shown on the network television news programs. I think eventually this trend of thinking developed among the people by the news programs must have its effect on the opinions of the "decision makers" as evidenced by the *New York Times* and the *Washington Post*, for example.

I definitely do not believe that we should have any form of federal censorship of network television news programs. I feel equally as strongly, however, that the National Administration as the leaders of the United States (the only national elected leaders we have) has an obligation to the American people to be continually conscious of the trend of thinking that is being caused and encouraged by the network news programs. It seems to me that the only way that the National Administration can be conscious of this trend is for the news programs to be recorded by some organization, for subject matter tapes to be made and to be available for review by many, many people including someone who would keep the National Administration informed of the trend of thinking that is being developed by the news which is being shown. It would then be the responsibility of the National Administration not to censor the news but to be sure that it understands what is taking place and then decide (as the leaders of the country) whether or not additional or possibly contradictory information is fully available. The National Administration has the responsibility of the American nation and the networks do not have.

I think that public opinion polls are useful to a National Administration, but I think it would be even more useful if a National Administration could be aware in advance of the development of the trends which will be reflected in future public opinion polls.

Our hope in trying to record and preserve the national network television news programs would be to make the information available for study by many people. We would hope that someone would study this material for the benefit of the National Administration in determining what courses they should take as the leaders of the country.

We note from newspaper accounts that President Nixon has removed from the White House the news teletype machines and the bank of three television monitors. We think that this is entirely correct, as we feel that any President must ignore the day by day reports on his or his administration's activity. We do not believe that you can really learn much about the trend of television news by watching an occasional daily news program. We do feel very strongly, however, that it is important that someone who is fully qualified keep the President and other members of the administration informed not as to what is being shown on television today necessarily, but as to the trend of the impact of what has been shown on television over the last days, weeks, or months.

We believe an administration will not be most effective unless it knows or at least has a good idea as to what the American people are thinking today and what they are seeing and hearing today which will affect their thinking tomorrow. *The Nashville Tennessean* of Jan. 31, 1969 publishes on page 10 a report by Joseph A. Loftis of the *New York Times* service on the Eisenhower Committee report. The last paragraph of this newspaper article states, "A task force on mass media and violence said studies indicate that 40% of the poor black children and 30% of the poor white children—compared with 15% of the middle class white children—believe that what they see on television represents an accurate portrayal of what life in America is all about."

We believe these percentage figures would be equally true (or larger) for adults. This means that a National Administration *must* be continually informed as to the continuing trend of impact of the television network news programs since they have the major national impact today.

I went to Washington in early November, and Pat Buchanan and I sat in his office and watched the whole tape. It became apparent to me during our conversation that somebody was going to make a speech using that scene of violence at the Democratic Convention that was shown three different times on NBC. I felt from what was said that it was going to be Vice-president Agnew.

The Vice-president did make a speech at the meeting of the Midwest Regional Republican Committee on November 13, 1969, using that scene of violence that was shown from three different angles as part of his criticism of the network news. I received a phone call from Pat Buchanan or someone in his office stating that Agnew had referred to that scene of violence being shown from three different angles and that Representative Bob Eckhardt of Texas ha questioned its accuracy. The Vice-president's press aide had then stated to the newsroom people that I was the one from whom they had gotten the information, so Pat Buchanan's office was calling to let me know that I'd probably be hearing from the press. Indeed, the Associated Press did call me. I confirmed that the Vice-president was correct in saying that NBC had shown the same scene of violence from three different camera angles. The networks were naturally quite disturbed by Agnew's remarks and reacted vigorously to defend their position.

The *Nashville Banner* ran an article entitled "Nashville Man Aided TV Attack." Of course, as I've said before, I was not really wanting to attack the networks, but it is true that without the Vanderbilt Television News Archive, there would be no way to verify that NBC had shown the same scene of violence from three different angles.

The speech and subsequent remarks by Vice-president Agnew, presidents of the networks, and other public figures lifted the questions about network news to national attention. As 1969 ended, the December 8 issue of *Broadcasting* pointed out that Vice-president Agnew's speech and the subsequent reactions may have brought renewed interest to the matter of videotaping network television news. We may have been unsuccessful in our efforts to gain the cooperation and assistance of the networks in 1969, but there was no doubt that we had gained their attention. On December 1, Senator Howard Baker had made a statement on the floor of the Senate calling for Congress to direct the Library of Congress to maintain tapes of the news programs. The interest and support we had secured from Senator Baker would prove to be of significant help to us in the years ahead, as we faced even more difficult challenges.

Chapter Three

What We've Begun We Must Continue:

Experimental Project Moves Toward Permanence

V anderbilt University was certainly aware that national interest in questions about television news had been heightened by the events of late 1969. Vanderbilt had made a cash contribution of $5,540 to the Archive in September of 1968, but its major contribution was in standing behind the project in the face of criticism from the networks. Many universities probably would not have continued their support. Vanderbilt made a further commitment to the Archive in early 1970 when the Board of Trust endorsed a three-year continuation of the project.

At its meeting on February 3, the Vanderbilt Board of Trust approved the general plan for a three-year continuation, including approval of me as unpaid administrative consultant and John DeWitt as unpaid technical consultant.

Responsibility for the project continued to be vested in the university committee, appointed by Chancellor Alexander Heard in 1968, with a smaller administrative committee made up of Robert McGaw, secretary of the university, Frank Grisham, representing the Joint University Libraries, and me as administrative consultant. The Archive still had no paid staff members.

Our belief that the Library of Congress was the best place for this project remained strong, but responses from the librarian of Congress stated that shortages of space and funding prevented taking on the project at this time. They did, however, emphasize their belief in the project's value. Senator Howard Baker was also committed to efforts to establish the project on a permanent basis at the Library of Congress, and he had drafted a proposed bill regarding this matter. Early in the year, Senator Baker wrote to each of the networks for their reactions to the bill. In a letter from NBC, Reuven Frank, president of NBC News, indicated that should the bill be enacted NBC would be pleased to cooperate by granting its consent to the Library of Congress to make recordings of its news programs and to permit students and others access to the recordings. He pointed out, however, that they would not grant consent for the Library of Congress to make copies of the tapes for others. Frank indicated that NBC's Law Department was concerned with the wording of part of the bill authorizing the librarian of Congress "to produce video tapes or films according to the subject matters of such telecasts." CBS also questioned the making of subject tapes in a letter from president Frank Stanton, indicating that they considered this provision "quite improper."

Lee Smith, Senator Howard Baker's legislative assistant, asked me to solicit the opinions of Vanderbilt's counsel as to the possible legal ramifications of enactment of the bill, and he also asked for the views of the general counsel of the Library of Congress copyright office. Smith learned that the general counsel of the copyright office felt that, while the newscasts were not copyrighted, the networks could assert property rights under the common law and that unauthorized copying of news program off the air would constitute a violation of those rights. However, L. Ray Patterson, professor of law at Vanderbilt, disagreed with that position. In a letter to Lee Smith, Patterson outlined the reasons for his position, stating that "even as to programs protected by statutory copyright, there is good argument that off-the-air taping of news programs does not infringe the copyright, so long as the copying is not done for commercial or competitive purposes." Patterson went on to say that since the networks erased the tapes, he believed they would have a difficult time arguing that their property interests were adversely affected, since the networks' practice of erasing the tapes would seem to "constitute an abandonment of any copyright interest."

The bill authorizing the Library of Congress to take over the Television News Archive was introduced in the spring of 1970. Over the course of the next few years, questions about the legal right of the Library of Congress or anyone else to continue this project would escalate.

In early 1970, I felt that there were two primary needs for the Archive: to acquire higher fidelity equipment for recording and to begin an index and abstracts to make the tapes we were recording more usable. On January 20, 1970, at a meeting in Chancellor Heard's office, Robert McGaw and I indicated our desire to put the project on a firmer basis to seek additional outside funding. Attending this meeting were Jack Massey and David K. (Pat) Wilson, who had provided financial support for the Archive, and Albert Menefee, a member of the board of the Justin and Valere Potter Foundation. These men offered to provide $75,000 toward the project, with half coming from Massey, through the Massey Foundation, and the other half from Wilson and Menefee, speaking for the Potter Foundation. This support was critical to the continuation and success of the Archive. In addition, it was their support that made it possible for us to accept a $125,000 matching grant from the Carthage Foundation later in the year. These financial contributions enabled us to buy our own equipment, hire some full-time staff members, and begin planning for indexing and abstracting the tapes.

Jack Massey and the Wilson family were very, very important to the success of the Archive. There's an interesting story about Jack Massey's support of the Archive. I heard that Jack was going to the White House to attend a dinner. I had already met Patrick Buchanan and been on friendly terms with him. So, I called Pat to see if he would ask President Nixon to tell Jack Massey how much we appreciated his support of the Archive's work. I heard nothing further about this matter until about a year later. One day, Jack was telling me about his and his wife's attending that dinner, and he said that in the receiving line the President had talked to him for so long that several people came to their dinner table to ask what the President had said. Well, that's what he was talking about—the Vanderbilt Archive. Jack continued to be a strong supporter, financial and otherwise, of the Archive over the years.

Naturally, however, we needed additional financial support to keep the project going. Following the Board of Trust's approval for a three-year continuation, I prepared the following document to help with further fund-raising efforts.

TELEVISION NEWS LIBRARY PROJECT
VANDERBILT UNIVERSITY,
NASHVILLE, TENNESSEE

April 7, 1970

Since August 5, 1968, Vanderbilt University has been tape recording from the air the three national network evening news programs. This has been done on a five day a week basis. The Republican and Democratic conventions of 1968 were also video tape recorded off the air from all three networks.

This recording has been done at the Joint University Library in Nashville, Tenn., under the direction of a committee appointed by Chancellor Alexander Heard. Robert A. McGaw, Secretary of Vanderbilt University, is Chairman of this Committee. The Director of the Joint University Library, Frank P. Grisham, is among the members of this committee.

This recording was undertaken because it was felt that these daily network news broadcasts were a unique record of the historical events of our time as well as a prime source for research for psychologists, sociologists, political scientists, economists, and historians. It was felt that just as libraries maintain newspaper and magazine collections, technology now permits the acquisition and maintenance of television news broadcasts.

Vanderbilt University undertook this project because it was not being done any where else. It was intended to demonstrate through the project that it could be done and that a national agency such as the Library of Congress could and should take over this task on a permanent and continuing basis.

We have kept and plan to keep the original tapes of each of the newscasts since August 5, 1968. We believe that subject matter tapes can and should be produced electronically from these original tapes.

We believe that these subject matter tapes can include on one tape all the material from a network covering a particular subject matter over a period of time without any alteration or change in such portions of the programs.

In order to prove to our satisfaction that such subject matter tapes could be electronically produced, we have made two subject matter tapes. The first subject matter tape was made from NBC's coverage of the Democratic convention on Wednesday night. We included in this 1 hour tape all scenes of demonstrations and violence shown by NBC that night and the comments from the floor of the convention concerning this violence.

The other subject matter tape covered NBC's daily news programs from August 5, 1968 through August 29, 1968. This tape included all material shown in this period of time concerning violence, demonstrations, and police activity. NBC was selected because it had, according to the ratings, the largest audience of any network on Wednesday night of the Democratic convention. Having selected NBC for the Wednesday night of the convention tape, we also selected them for the August tape.

A very thorough study of these two subject matter tapes has clearly convinced us that such subject matter tapes on many major subjects would be of extreme interest and should be available in many libraries throughout the United States. The network news programs need and deserve thorough and complete study by many scholars and other interested people.

We have secured from interested foundations and individuals here in Nashville $75,000 to cover one half of the cost of equipment and one year of operation of the project including the cost of indexing and the cost of making subject matter tapes. We are planning to buy the necessary equipment, set up the office and staff as soon as possible, hoping that we will be able to secure the necessary additional financing from interested sources out of Nashville. The annual budget will be $105,000 per year for three years with an additional $55,000 required during the first year for equipment.

Believing that this project is so important for the present and for the future, we are purchasing new equipment which will enable us to place on each picture as it is video tape recorded the name of the Network, the date and the time. The recording itself will be done by very much better equipment which will result in an improved quality. We also plan to develop an Indexing System and an Index. In addition, subject matter tapes on the major subjects covered in the network news programs will be completed on a continuous basis.

We hope that eventually copies of at least the subject matter tapes will be available in many libraries throughout the United States. This, we believe, will result in the network news programs receiving the thorough and comprehensive study which we think they deserve, both now and in the future.

Much of my time in 1970 was spent in fund-raising activities for the Archive. Perhaps the most significant aspect of my 1970 fund-raising efforts, however, had actually been set in motion in 1969 when I had visited with Patrick Buchanan at the White House. At that time, Buchanan had introduced me to someone in charge of fund-raising. I specifically asked for help in giving me names of people who might be interested in putting some money into the archiving of television news. Over the course of time, they did give me some names, and I made a number of trips to visit with people who might be interested.

One of these trips was to California, where I followed up on appointments set up for me by the White House. I contacted one individual in Los Angeles and two in San Francisco. I contacted a lady, whose name I do not now recall, who lived on the campus of a school in the Los Angeles area. I knew that she had the potential to make a contribution since I noticed on her wall pictures of a number of buildings that she and her late husband had funded for various universities. This lady believed strongly that network news programs were having an adverse effect on the country, and she wanted this fact stressed. At that time, I did not feel that the Archive should stress this aspect, so I did not follow up in requesting funds from her.

During our meeting, she requested that I call on a certain organization in Los Angeles; she phoned to make an appointment for me to talk with the head of the organization in his office that evening. When I called at the office, I was told that he was busy, so I sat down in the lobby to wait. While I was waiting, several police officers rushed in and went into the gentleman's office; then all of them, the police officers and the head of the organization, rushed from the office and left the building. Under the circumstances, I felt it was wise for me to leave, too, and I did so, as I really knew nothing at all about this organization.

On this same trip to California, I was attending a company meeting in San Francisco. While there, I called on Mr. Jaquelin Hume and Mr. Dudley Swim, both of whom at that time were members of Governor Ronald Reagan's "Kitchen Cabinet." These appointments were arranged for me by the man I had met in the White House in 1969, and the Vanderbilt Archive did receive a contribution of $500 from each of these men.

Hume suggested that I visit with Dr. Glenn Campbell, who was director of the Hoover Institution at Stanford University. I did go down to Stanford and had a very nice visit with Campbell and other members of the staff of the Hoover Institution. I explained to them fully the Archive's operation and followed up this visit later with other contacts and special efforts to make the material in the Television News Archive easily available on request to their institution.

I visited with several other foundations and individuals throughout the United States, including some in New York and Connecticut, but was unsuccessful in securing additional funding. The Archive did receive a contribution of $1,000 from Sam Fleming, a Nashville business executive.

In late July of 1970, however, the Archive had a visit from R. Daniel McMichael of the Mellon Foundation/Scaife Family Charitable Trusts. This first visit by Dan McMichael proved to be the beginning of a long and important relationship with the Scaife Foundations. McMichael made a number of valuable suggestions and comments and asked us to send him some figures regarding the costs for continuing the project. This contact eventually led to a $125,000 matching grant from the Carthage Foundation, one of the Scaife Family Charitable Foundations. I'm not even sure I knew at the time how this contact originated, but later while reading *Richard Nixon's Secret Files*, edited by Bruce

Oudes, I found that it was probably a direct result of my asking the White House for help and of their interest in seeing that the news programs were being kept somewhere.

I had no compunction at all in requesting assistance for the Archive from President Nixon's administration or later from President Carter's administration. I had learned by that time that the very foundation of the evening network news programs was the President and also his relationship with Congress. I found that it was an exception if there was any evening news program that did not feature a reference to the President's activities.

We continued during this time our efforts to make the Vanderbilt Television News Archive more useful by indexing and abstracting the tapes. During the summer of 1970, three graduate students in the Peabody Library School, under the direction of Mr. Wilburn Clouse, worked to devise some guidelines to follow in indexing the video tapes. They submitted some excellent plans and recommendations, but due to technical difficulties and financial problems, their recommendations were not followed completely. We realized that we would have to develop our own system for indexing and that this would be the first priority and responsibility of the Archive's new administrator when he or she was appointed.

Another important aspect of the events of 1970 that needs to be mentioned is Chancellor Alexander Heard's continuing support and encouragement, without which the Archive could not have continued. Although Chancellor Heard had been a firm supporter of the project from the very beginning, in 1970 he also had a personal experience that helped to convince him that what was reported in television news should be kept on record.

During the year, Chancellor Heard was asked by President Nixon to give him a report and advice concerning the disorders on college campuses throughout the United States. NBC News carried a story one night that in his report Chancellor Heard had stated that college campuses were dying and that he had made particular mention of Columbia University. I saw this story on NBC in my home that night. The next morning, I called the Archive and asked them to make a transcript of that story on NBC News and deliver it to the chancellor's office because I felt that I knew Chancellor Heard well enough to know that he would never have made a statement indicating that college campuses were dying. I also knew he would have been very unlikely to have made such a statement about Columbia University since there had been talk in the Nashville news media that Heard was being considered for president of that university.

I never discussed this matter personally with Chancellor Heard, but I did see on the next evening's NBC Nightly News a correction of the story (this was a very, very rare occurrence for the network news to admit that they had aired incorrect information). I later understood that the chancellor had called NBC about their report and in the course of the conversation had referred to having before him a transcript of what was said. I've always felt that, had the Archive not existed and had the chancellor not had a transcript of the actual program, NBC could have questioned whether or not he correctly heard what was in the report. I think this incident did more than anything else could have to convince Heard of the importance of having actual video tapes of the network news on record. I never heard Chancellor Heard speak of any bias (liberal or conservative) in the network news. I know that he did refer frequently to the importance of network news being on record just as newspapers and magazines had always been on record.

College campuses were, of course, in turmoil at this time, and 1970 was the year protest activity reached a violent climax at Kent State and other campuses. When I saw the coverage on NBC of the Kent State incident involving the shooting by National Guard troops of several students, I felt that NBC had presented a four-minute segment that would almost assuredly stir up other campuses throughout the country. The segment included a picture of a female student bending over the body of a dead student on the ground. The picture stayed on the screen with no sound or comment for the longest time I've ever seen the television screen alive but with no sound. The silence attracted the viewer's attention more than anything else could have. There was also a very tearful interview with the father of one of the students killed at Kent State. Following the Kent State incident, there was later violence at Jackson, Mississippi, resulting in the deaths of two students at Jackson State College.

My concern over this representation, as well as my continuing concern over the matter of the news media reporting controversial remarks by prominent people out of context, led me to write a letter to Governor William Scranton, who was then chairman of the Presidential Commission on Campus Unrest.

July 24, 1970

Governor William Scranton, Chairman
Presidential Commission on Campus Unrest
1717 H Street, N.W. - Ninth Floor
Washington, D.C.

Dear Governor Scranton:

I am very much interested in the purpose of your Commission and in your hearings and investigations. I note that the newspapers indicate that you will advise the President, if you so find, that he should silence the rhetoric of Vice-President Agnew. I also note that you plan hearings and investigations on the violence at Kent State and Jackson, Mississippi.

In your investigation as to the effect, if any, on campus violence of the "rhetoric" of Vice-President Agnew, I would like to raise the following questions: How many of these people commenting on the Vice-President's rhetoric have actually read one or more of his talks in their entirety? Are they talking about the Vice-President's rhetoric or about the way in which parts of the Vice-President's talks have been presented by the news media? Has controversy been stimulated not by what the Vice-President has had to say, particularly when considered in relation to his entire talk, or has it been stimulated by the news media's practice of extracting the most controversial parts of his talk from the rest of the talk and then emphasizing this controversial part?

Over a period of time does what a prominent person said gradually become obscured and replaced in the news media by what others say he said?

I think the fact that this can be done and is frequently done is emphasized by the enclosed copy of an article in "U.S. News and World Report" under date of March 9, 1970. When the Chief Justice of the Supreme Court of the United States makes statements such as this, there must be some justification.[1]

I think it is vitally important to remember that news media have generally acknowledged that they are interested in the abnormal and controversial. This is the part of any speech that is emphasized by the news media, particularly television, since it is so limited in the time and space available to it. I think this is clearly indicated in the television coverage in the National news programs of your hearings of the past week. I suspect that a complete report of your remarks concerning the type of report that you would make to the President concerning Vietnam and the Vice-President's rhetoric might give a different picture from that presented by the news media.

I think in your investigation at Kent State and Jackson, Mississippi it is important to determine what actually took place. However, what actually took place

---

[1] In the *U. S. News and World Report*'s "People of the Week" column for March 9, 1970, Chief Justice Warren Burger's policy of barring television and radio coverage of his public appearance except under prearranged, limited conditions was reported. The article quotes Chief Justice Burger as saying he "'didn't want some TV editor to take a lurid phrase' out of context and put it on the air." (Author's comment, 1995)

is not necessarily the important thing so far as the effect of Kent State and Jackson, Mississippi on violence on other campuses. What is important in determining the effect of Kent State and Jackson, Mississippi on violence on other campuses is what the students of these other campuses "thought" took place at Kent State and Jackson. What they thought took place was determined by what they saw or read in the National news media. It was particularly influenced by what they saw on television and how what they saw was presented.

It would seem to me that a study of the effect of Kent State and Jackson on campus disorders throughout the Country would need to include how National television news programs presented Kent State and Jackson. I would very much hope that your Commission would be able to make a study of how the network news programs covered Kent State and Jackson with particular emphasis on the three major evening news programs.

It seems to me that we are faced today, when you consider any type of National violence, with two questions: what actually took place and what people understood took place and how the event is presented in the news. These are not necessarily always completely the same. [2]

---

[2] A reading of the Scranton Commission report on Kent State gives a different picture from that presented by the networks. For example, the networks referred to Kent State as a peaceful campus where the worst thing that had happened was a "panty raid." The Scranton Commission report indicates that there had been violence and violent protests, including the burning of the National Guard Armory. (Author's comment, 1995)

At the Joint University Library here on the Vanderbilt University campus, we have been video taping the three National Network News programs since August 5, 1968. We have done this because it was not being done elsewhere. We video tape this material from the air, and because of financial limitations, have had to use inexpensive equipment. (We are now arranging for much better equipment and better trained personnel.) Because of these limitations in equipment we have very occasionally missed parts of some programs. We do have a great deal of information on video tape on Kent State and Jackson and on the Vice-President's speeches. We should be glad for your Commission to avail itself of any information we have.

Sincerely,
Paul C. Simpson

PCS:lt
cc: Mr. John Gaventa

I received a reply from John J. Kirby, Jr., deputy director of the President's Commission on Campus Unrest, thanking us for our interest and offer of assistance. However, due to time constraints, the Commission determined that they would not study the tapes of national network news. Kirby's letter reminded me again how important it was to index and abstract the tapes to make them truly useful.

Later in 1970, Vice-president Agnew again called attention to national television news when he made a speech at the Associated Press Managing Editors Convention in Honolulu on November 20, 1970. What interested me about this speech was how it was reported by the networks. In the course of his speech, Agnew referred to some of the problems with the network news. When it was reported on television, commentators reported that Agnew said that in his opinion the American news media was the fairest and finest in the world. This portrayal showed me once again that people can't depend on what they hear on television news to tell them what someone said because it may or it may not be complete or accurate.

I later referred to Vice-president Agnew's speech when I talked to a joint meeting of two political science classes at the request of the professors. I referred to the speech and the report in the *New York Times*, which stated that the Vice-president had been critical of the network news but had then said it was still the fairest and finest in the world. The network news programs, on the other hand, had not reported about Agnew's making any critical remarks but had simply reported that Agnew said in Honolulu that American television news was the fairest and finest in the world. I used this comparison to point out to the classes the inadvisability of depending just on television news to tell them what a person had said. I encouraged them to seek out several sources in order to be sure that they knew all that the person had said.

Using as an illustration a Vanderbilt Divinity School story that criticized President Nixon for attacking "dissenting students," I also pointed out to them what happened when a person or a news organization depended on the national television news to tell them what someone had said. This story was based on something that the national news media had reported at the time of the anti-Vietnam demonstrations in Washington, D.C. They reported that Nixon had awakened in the middle of the night and had made a trip over to the Lincoln Memorial, where he talked to some of the demonstrators. He criticized the college students who were "burning down campuses." This episode was heavily reported in the national news media, stating that the President criticized "dissenting students" rather than stating that he criticized "students who were burning down campuses."

This reinforced a conclusion that I had reached that a national figure would be treated by the news media as follows: the President of the United States could usually, but not always, depend on the news media to report what he had said. Any other national figure would probably be quoted only if he made a statement with pithy or controversial remarks that could be extracted from their full context and reported. If he made a calm, reasoning speech, it would probably not be reported. This action is a result of the networks' seeking what Fred Friendly stated in his book was necessary to have a successful news program: "conviction, controversy, and a point of view."

Following my talk to the political science classes, I was asked if I didn't call primarily on conservative people and organizations for financial support for the Archive. I responded that I did because conservatives generally felt that the national news media was dominated by liberal people who presented their "conviction" and "point of view," and they were disturbed by this fact. Someone then asked what I would have done if it had been the liberals who were disturbed by the network news. I responded that I would then have called on the liberals for financial support, believing I would have secured it under those circumstances. I learned rather early that an approach based just on the scholastic value of having these materials preserved and available for study wouldn't get me very far in fund-raising. The reason for this theory was that at that time, most people were not interested in studying anything other than print material. They really felt that spoken words and pictures (television) had no impact. The reason for that feeling was that most of the tenured professors had spent their lives studying print material, were comfortable studying print material, and felt that it was the only important material to study. Also, most educational institutions were always looking for money for their own purposes.

By the end of 1970, the financial situation for the Archive was looking much brighter that it had at the beginning of the year. We had completed installation of approximately $50,000 worth of the best videotape recording equipment available and had begun hiring staff members. Rebecca Shull, the first staff member hired, served as administrative assistant for the Archive and also worked with me to start abstracting some of the programs. Later, Aaron Burleson was hired as electronics technician to help with the taping. With the awarding of the Carthage Foundation grant and the receipt of the first of these funds in December, we were ready to hire the Archive's first full-time administrator and develop the much-needed system of indexing and data retrieval.

Chapter Four

Why Are They So Fearful?:

Networks' Concern About News Archive Project Grows

A s 1971 began, the Vanderbilt Television News Archive had a valuable collection of about 1,500 hours of videotaped recordings of the network evening newscasts dating back to August 5, 1968. However, the collection was not fully usable unless the user knew exactly what he wanted and the date and the network on which the news had been shown. The Archive had two staff members, and their offices and the equipment were located in one fairly small room off the second floor hall of the main library. By the end of the year, the Archive had made major strides in terms of becoming a truly valuable research collection.

The first significant step forward for the Archive in terms of making it more useful was the installation of new equipment at the end of 1970. As of January 1, 1971, following Bob McGaw's suggestion, the video tapes themselves were electronically imprinted with the network, date, and a running clock time (changing at ten second intervals). This step was critical because it would make items easy to find once an index was developed. As mentioned earlier, developing a system of indexing was to be the top priority for the new administrator, who was hired early in 1971.

The Vanderbilt University News Bureau issued the following press release to announce both the awarding of the Carthage Foundation grant and the hiring of James P. Pilkington as the Archive's first full-time administrator.

Vanderbilt Television News Archive
Gets $125,000 Grant

A grant of $125,000 has been awarded to Vanderbilt University by the Carthage Foundation of Pittsburgh, Pa., in support of the university's Television News Archive now in its third year.

The archive is a permanent collection of videotapes of the daily news broadcasts of the three national television networks. Vanderbilt began the project in August 1968 with the idea of making the national news telecasts permanently accessible for reference and analysis.

Primary funding of the Television News Archive so far has come from the Jack C. Massey Foundation and the Justin and Valere Potter Foundation, both of Nashville.

The Carthage Foundation stipulated that its $125,000 grant be divided evenly during 1971 between operating expenses for continued taping, and the development of a much needed system of indexing and data retrieval.

The project was originally conceived by Paul C. Simpson, a Vanderbilt law graduate who is an insurance company executive in Nashville. Simpson knew that surveys indicate that more Americans rely on television for their knowledge of the world than on any other source of information, and he ascertained that no complete and permanent record of network newscasts was being kept by the networks or anyone else. The high cost of videotape, storage and staff had discouraged the making and keeping of any such file.

Simpson is Vanderbilt's administrative consultant for the archive and member of a three-man administrative committee along with Robert A. McGaw, secretary of the university, and Frank P. Grisham, director of the Joint University Libraries. Jack DeWitt, who retired in 1968 as president of WSM, Inc., is technical consultant.

The archive is housed in the general library building of the Joint University Libraries, which represent the combined book, periodical and other document holdings of Vanderbilt University, George Peabody College for Teachers and Scarritt College, all situated in the University Center of Nashville.

James P. Pilkington was recently appointed administrator of the Television News Archive. Other members of the full-time staff are Miss Rebecca Shull, administrative assistant, and Aaron Burleson, electronics technician.

Pilkington earned two degrees in English at Vanderbilt in 1945 and 1946, and from 1947 to 1970 was with the Methodist Publishing House. He researched and wrote the award-winning history of the first century of American Methodist publishing and was responsible for the firm's 60,000 volume library and for the development of a quarterly index to all periodical publications of the denomination.

It will be Pilkington's task to devise a way of efficiently indexing the television newscasts so that the videotapes can be easily researched.

He sees the Television News Archive as the pioneer venture into a new field based on a new way of thinking, that of considering the spoken word and visual image of television as documents in the same sense as are the written and printed word.

"The Vanderbilt videotapes date back to the Republican and Democratic nominating conventions of 1968, farther than any such collection in the country. They are of fundamental significance to the objective study of television and its impact," said Pilkington.

The index for the archive will be produced in accord with such recognized news indexing standards as those employed in the New York Times Index. "But," Pilkington said, "classifying television news is more complex because we must index for both the senses, sight and hearing."

The archive was recently equipped with new high fidelity videotaping equipment at a cost of approximately $50,000. The cost of raw tape alone sometimes exceeds $100 a day, according to officials.

In addition to the expense of tape, everything must be done in threes. The daily network newscasts are on the air in Nashville at the same time, and it is necessary to have electronic equipment in triplicate in order to record the programs.

Each evening, the 30-minute newscasts by NBC, CBS and ABC are captured in black and white for posterity by a process which records electrical impulses on magnetic tape. It is not a photographic process.

The Television News Archive records the telecasts as they come over the air, and imprints electronically on every frame the network, the date and the time to the nearest ten seconds.

The recording machines can also make copies of the tapes, and procedures are being developed whereby other institutions and scholars might secure copies. Already the archive has proved useful in several studies made by Vanderbilt faculty and students and by researchers outside of Nashville.

Hiring Jim Pilkington was one of the Archive's major steps responsible for its being successful and still being around today. Jim, the ideal choice for that job, was very service-oriented and was largely responsible for building the reputation that the Archive has today: being very helpful to people and wanting to give them good service. He did an excellent job with his staff and the students who worked with the Archive. It was certainly a real bonus that the Archive was located on the Vanderbilt campus in the library because we could work with students or former students with the education and interest to make them realize that they were engaged in something new, different, and important. Many of them really went beyond the call of duty in their jobs. Jim worked well with all types of people and did a fine job supervising their activities and the activities of the Archive.

We were a good team—Jim as full-time administrator and I as unpaid administrative consultant. Jim would look at the Archive strictly from the standpoint of the person and the service they wanted. I would look at it from the standpoint of "Can we afford it? Is it a precedent we want to set? Could it give us a problem with the networks or legal problems of any kind?" Jim was an excellent person. He and I worked together, with Jim doing most of the real work but with our talking about it. We went to lunch practically everyday and talked about the Archive.

I had enough personnel headaches of my own at that time, because I was still working at Metropolitan Life. When you employ forty salespeople, four or five assistants, and ten or fifteen clerical people, you've all the personnel you want to supervise. So I made it clear to Jim from the very beginning that I didn't want to have anything to do with personnel. I didn't want him to think I was going to try to run the day-to-day operations at the Archive. I said, "I'm going to try very hard when I want somebody here to do something to ask you to ask them to do it. I may not always be successful in that endeavor, but that's what I'm going to try."

We had an excellent working relationship. One of our first major projects surfaced in the spring of 1971. I received a call from the Republican National Committee. That call was followed by a March 9, 1971, letter from Bob Dole, who was chairman of the committee at that time. The committee wanted to know if we could compile and show some tapes of all newscasts or commentaries about the Laotian incursion. They were interested in newscasts aired between February 1 and March 4, 1971. Jim and I together went through the coverage of NBC and CBS for that period of time and made a list of the items to be put on the tapes. Although we had tapes of the ABC newscasts also, we were having some problems with the equipment that day, so we felt we should start with the two networks that had the largest viewing audience according to the ratings. Because of time limitations and equipment problems, we were never able to include any of the ABC coverage.

We completed the compiled tapes of the CBS and NBC coverage. We didn't do any study of the material; we just completed the tapes. The night before I was to show the tapes of the Laos incursion in a hearing room in the Senate Office Building, the Republicans announced the showing. Senator Clifford Hansen was listed as sponsor. A copy of that notice went to every senator and representative's office and to everyone in the news media. Everybody, including the news media, knew that I was to be there.

When I arrived the next morning, Bob Schieffer, a CBS correspondent, was there and stayed the whole time. We had senators, members of the House of Representatives, and others stop by for a short period of time to watch the tapes. I showed the tapes, with a minimum amount of comment except to state that we had simply compiled items about the Laotian incursion which were shown by CBS and NBC between February 1 and March 4, 1971. I also read the following statement, which we had recently prepared to be read at all showings of videotapes from the Archive.

STATEMENT TO BE READ AT SHOWINGS OF VIDEOTAPES FROM THE VANDERBILT TELEVISION NEWS ARCHIVE

The Vanderbilt Television News Archive, begun in August, 1968, is a permanent collection of the daily news broadcasts of the three national television networks, held for the sole purpose of making the national news telecasts permanently accessible for reference and research.

Administered through the Joint University Libraries, an enterprise of Vanderbilt University, George Peabody College, and Scarritt College, all located in Nashville, Tennessee, the Television News Archive makes its collection available to users on a loan basis only, for stated charges covering service expenses.

None of its materials is to be recorded on audio or video tapes and none is to be rebroadcast over radio or television.

Beyond technical necessities and such cataloging or indexing processes basic to the use of the material, the Archive does not involve itself in the content of the material in the collection. The Archive is not responsible for opinions and/or judgments respecting this content that might be expressed by those using it.

The Archive is made possible through grants of funds from individuals and foundations believing it to be a worthwhile service.

While I was showing the tapes in Washington that morning, Jim Pilkington received a phone call in Nashville from CBS's assistant bureau chief in Washington, Don Richardson. Richardson asked Jim who had given me permission to bring those tapes to Washington. I think that what he meant to ask was, "Did CBS give their permission for the tapes to be shown?" At first he just asked who had given me permission. Later in their conversation, Richardson specifically asked Jim if CBS and NBC had given their permission for the tapes to be made and shown. Jim referred him to me on this question since I had been the one in contact with the networks since 1968. Jim's notes about this conversation state that "The conversation ended with pleasantries, but it was evident that Mr. Richardson was conserned (sic) with the matter of permissions and by what authority the University and Mr. Simpson were doing this."

After Richardson's conversation with Vanderbilt, the bureau manager for CBS News in Washington, William J. Small, called me. I left the tape running as I talked to him on the phone in the Senate hearing room. He said something negative to me several times about showing copyrighted material without permission. Although I may have expressed my feelings more strongly, I basically replied that, "This material, in our opinion, is not copyrighted." In fact, at that time the news programs were not copyrighted, a situation that would change in a few years. We talked for some time; I told him the Archive would be glad to send him the tapes when I returned to Nashville. In the course of the conversation, I thought, "Why should I lug those heavy boxes back to Nashville with me?" So I told him if he'd send someone over who I would recognize, that I would give that person the tapes. Late that afternoon, a CBS correspondent whom I recognized from seeing him on television did arrive; I gave him the tapes.

Just before lunch, Bob Schieffer had asked me if I was going to be back after lunch. I told him yes and asked why he wanted to know. He said the network wanted a story for the CBS Evening News and wanted a picture of me showing the tapes. After lunch, the network crew came into the hearing room with their then-heavy equipment and cables and set up to take pictures of me showing the tapes. Afterwards, Schieffer asked me to come out into the hallway of the Senate Office Building and do a stand-up interview with him. I understand he also did an interview with Senator Hansen. My major comments in the interview with Schieffer concerned why I thought it important to have this material available, both for now and into the future, for the American people to study. That was the main idea I emphasized. I did not make any kind of remarks about whether the networks were biased. I didn't make any remarks about the tapes that we were showing that day, except that they were tapes of the incursion.

About 4:30, while I was showing the tapes, I noticed that Schieffer went to the phone in the hearing room and returned beaming and looking pleased. Then he told me we were going to be on the Cronkite Show that night. At that time, a correspondent received a $500 bonus if one of his stories was on the air. I understand that the practice of paying a bonus was later discontinued. Any correspondent is naturally pleased when his story is going to be aired, and Bob Schieffer was pleased as he told me that we were going to be on Cronkite.

I watched the Cronkite news in the airport that night on the way home, but the story wasn't shown. Instead, there was a more than three-minute segment about the difficulty of keeping accurate time on the clocks in the towers of London and about the person charged with that responsibility [see Appendix B, Abstracts for the CBS News on that day]. This was obviously a timeless fill-in piece that could be used at the last minute when the producer in New York decided it should be substituted for a story that for some reason the network didn't wish to run. The bureau manager in Washington thought our story was going to be run, and he had told Schieffer that it would be, but when it came time to make the final decisions, I think the New York executives decided that CBS shouldn't give the Archive any publicity. That explanation has to be the only reason for their not showing it. Any technical difficulties, for example, would undoubtedly have been discovered before the CBS executive in Washington talked with Schieffer late that afternoon.

The last-minute removal of this item by the executive producer in New York gave me definite proof of the power and authority of the executive producer. In this case, both the correspondent and the bureau manager in Washington had thought that this item was worthy of showing to the American people. I then realized that regardless of the number of people working on television news programs, in the final analysis, the "conviction" and "point of view" of one man in New York, the executive producer, would determine what the American people saw and heard. This incident also led me to understand why a correspondent who wanted his stories on the air would soon learn what the "conviction" and "point of view" of the executive producer were and make every effort to make his news items agree with that "conviction" and "point of view."

I never asked Schieffer or anyone else at CBS about why our story wasn't shown, but my belief that the network didn't want to give the Archive any publicity is completely reinforced by the fact that in all these years they never have given any. To my knowledge, none of the networks has ever mentioned the name of the Vanderbilt Television News Archive on the air.

Again, the showing of the tapes stirred up controversy nationally as well as locally. Senator Bill Brock was quoted in the March 14, 1971, Nashville *Tennessean* as saying the network coverage of the Laotian incursion showed "a common thread of bias" against the Nixon administration. An article in the previous day's *Nashville Banner* reported that Senator Clifford Hansen and Senator Robert Dole agreed with Brock that the network reports reflected bias. The *Tennessean* report also quoted Richard Salant, president of CBS News, as saying, "We want to see the tapes shown in Washington because they were not shown with the permission of CBS." (As noted above, CBS did pick up these tapes on the day of the showing.)

Vanderbilt's student newspaper, *The Vanderbilt Hustler*, ran an editorial criticizing the university for allowing me to take the tapes to Washington. Of course, the anti-Vietnam sentiment on Vanderbilt's campus was just as strong as it was on other campuses at that time, so I think that's the reason the students were objecting. No one in the Vanderbilt administration ever made any criticism of me for taking those tapes to Washington.

In his March, 1971, report to the people of Tennessee, Senator Howard Baker wrote, "Regardless of which side of the controversy one takes—and few are neutral on the issue—the controversy only heightens the need for preservation of the TV news programs for purposes of research and study." Senator Baker continued his efforts to have the Archive become a project of the Library of Congress, and because no action had been taken on the bill introduced by Senator Baker in the spring of 1970, he reintroduced the bill on March 10, 1971.

An article in the April 1, 1971, issue of the Washington *Evening Star* referred to me as the "man in the middle" of a political squabble, not a very comfortable place to be. Throughout the controversy, I continued to emphasize that the Archive's role was simply in making the tapes available and that we had made no comment regarding the content of the newscasts. I found it difficult to understand how CBS could possibly object to showing in the Office Building of the Senate of the United States material which CBS had already shown to over twenty million Americans. We could not show anything other than that which CBS had chosen to show since the only material we had was a video tape of the CBS Evening News.

As I mentioned earlier, we had given the tapes to CBS in Washington, and they returned them several weeks later with no comment whatsoever. We also later sent the tapes to NBC for their review. Although we never received any comment directly from NBC, Reuven Frank, president of NBC News, did refer to my giving him the tapes in a speech on May 5 at the University of Missouri. I wanted the networks to have the tapes and see what we were doing partly because I was still hoping to gain their cooperation. We continued our efforts in 1971 to obtain copies of the logs from the networks to help in developing an index, but none of the networks ever agreed to provide us with copies of their logs. We did have regular correspondence with CBS News President Richard Salant, who at one point agreed to provide copies of transcripts of the CBS Evening News, "so long as they are for your use only and are not to be given redistribution outside your Archive." However, this offer of assistance never materialized.

The spring of 1971 was a busy time at the Archive. Requests for services continued to grow. One of the people with whom I had talked in Washington about the services provided by the Archive was Arthur Rowse, research director of the "Study of News Media" for the Twentieth Century Fund. Rowse was directing a study focused on the issue of news control—the extent to which major wire services and networks dominated the daily flow of news in the United States. He was very interested in the work of the Archive and wanted to see some specific program segments which would help support and document their own research.

In addition to the "Statement to Be Read at Showings of Videotapes From the Vanderbilt Television News Archive," we developed a number of other policies for the Archive in the spring of 1971, including a statement of the "Purpose of the Archive," a policy on the "Use of Materials," a "Loan Agreement," and a "Schedule of Charges for Services." Jim Pilkington and I had immediately started to work on the question of how to go about indexing this complicated collection, and we tried to gather as much information as we could to help us. In late March, 1971, we visited New York to talk with the *New York Times* Index staff about our plans, and they were very helpful. We had also written to Frank Stanton, president of CBS, to request a meeting with someone in their archive.

Dr. Frank Stanton, President, CBS, Inc.
51 West 52nd Street
New York, New York

Dear Dr. Stanton:

I am enclosing copy of our letter of January 20, 1969 and a news item from Vanderbilt University which was released last week.

The purpose in sending these two items is to try to give you an idea as to the activity here at the Joint University Libraries.

Under the terms of the Carthage Foundation, half of the grant is to be expended for the development of a much needed system of indexing and data retrieval. James Pilkington and I are coming to New York on March 30 and are planning to talk with the *New York Times* indexing people on April 1. We would very much like to have the opportunity on March 31 to talk with someone in your library concerning this question of indexing and retrieval.

We are very anxious to get all the information possible to help us in working out a competent indexing and retrieval system.

We would appreciate it if you would ask the proper person in your organization to contact us so that a definite appointment can be made, hopefully on March 31. Or if you would ask someone to give us the name of the proper person, we will be glad to contact them from here.

Thank you very much.

Sincerely yours,

Paul C. Simpson
Administrative Consultant

PCS/mc
March 19, 1971

During our trip to New York, we did visit CBS, as well as the other two networks, to discuss the question of how to index the videotape collection. On this same trip, Jim and I also stopped in Washington, where we met briefly with John Marsh, a lawyer who had been recommended to us by Dan McMichael. Because CBS continued to be so negative about what we were doing, we had discussed the situation with McMichael, who suggested we talk with John Marsh about the copyright issue. Marsh was very interested in our project and in the negative responses from the networks. After we returned to Nashville, Robert McGaw followed up our visit by sending Marsh copies of the opinions of the general counsel of the Copyright Office and of Ray Patterson, a member of the Vanderbilt Law School faculty.

We continued talking with numerous people about the problem of indexing television news, and we came to the conclusion that the only way to do the index was to first complete the abstracts and then index to the abstract. The index would lead a researcher from the index to the abstracts to the tapes as the primary source material. Nothing like this had ever been developed; it wasn't an easy system to come up with.

We prepared a sample index and abstracts for the first two weeks of May, 1971, to be circulated to selected individuals and organizations for review and comment. Since it was the Carthage Foundation grant that had made it possible, the first copy sent outside the walls of Vanderbilt went to Dan McMichael and Richard Scaife of the Scaife Family Charitable Trusts. We wanted them to have a chance to survey the index and abstracts and to think about them before we even sent them to anyone else. We later sent copies of this sample index and abstracts to about thirty reference librarians and other professionals with whom we had worked, including people responsible for the *New York Times Index,* the *Wall Street Journal Index,* and the archives of the three networks. By the end of the year, we had begun investigating possibilities for computerization. We approached a Nashville firm which specialized in computer work about putting the index and abstracts on computer. After we had a number of conversations with them, they spent some time studying the matter and informed us that they did not think the computerization could be accomplished successfully at that time. I later felt that we were very fortunate that we did not try to put the material on computer at that time.

The development of the index and abstracts was a significant step for the Archive. As Jim Pilkington put it in a cover letter when he sent the index to Jack Massey, "we think it is interesting just to see the TV news boiled down and solidified into something you can hold in your hand." This "solidification" was, of course, the step which made the Archive truly useful as a research collection.

The Archive expanded physically during 1971 as well by first expanding into the hallway, where we had a desk for the secretary. Then we took a room that had once been a ladies' lounge and made it into the equipment room where we did the taping and technical work. Aaron Burleson left the Archive in the spring, and Ronald Moulton was hired as the new electronics technician in June, 1971. Ron was a major contributor to the continued success of the Archive. We were beginning to be more well-known nationally as well as locally, and requests for service were increasing.

Jim Pilkington prepared a written document entitled "The Year 1971," which outlined the significant progress made during that year. Over half of the collection had been abstracted by that time, and we added a fourth staff member, Skip Pfeiffer, to index. The employment of Pfeiffer was another major favorable step for the Archive. Skip did a fine job as indexer and was still doing the indexing in 1994. The fact that the same person did the indexing over many years gave a continuity to the index that it would not have had if there had been five or six different people involved. With these steps, we were ready to begin publication of the index and abstracts on a monthly schedule beginning in January, 1972.

The year ended on a relatively stable note. The calm, however, was not to last. A premonition of this storm perhaps arrived in a November 10 memorandum from Ray Patterson, professor of law, to Chancellor Alexander Heard. While attending the International Conference of States on the Protection of Phonograms, Patterson had discussed the Vanderbilt Television News Archive with Robert V. Evans, vice-president and general counsel of CBS. Patterson's memorandum indicated that Evans "made clear that while CBS did not like it, he had no intention of allowing them to take any action. He said, 'We are turning our heads,' but I suspect they are, in fact, keeping a very close watch."

Patterson was right that CBS was keeping a close watch on the activities of the Archive, as we were soon to learn.

Although there had been hints before, the CBS network's first unequivocal statement that they considered what we were doing a violation of their copyright came in the spring of 1972. After reviewing responses to the sample index in 1971, we prepared the Archive's first official *Television News Index and Abstracts* for the month of January, 1972. This publication was sent to a selected list of individuals and organizations without charge, as it was still in an experimental stage. This mailing was partly a marketing tool. We realized that we couldn't put a new product on the market and expect to receive many requests for it when nobody knew anything about it. My feeling was that we had to let people know what television news indexing and abstracting was. Then, once they saw what it was and became accustomed to it, they would want to subscribe.

We sent a free subscription to the *Index and Abstracts* to approximately 250 interested people and organizations. Among those were the three networks. Robert V. Evans, vice-president and general counsel of CBS, responded in an April 4, 1972, letter, "Without questioning the purpose of the Index, I must advise you that your recording of our broadcasts off-the-air without permission constitutes a clear infringement of our common law copyright in such broadcasts." Evans pointed out that, in an effort to avoid litigation, CBS would like to discuss the possibility of offering the Archive a royalty-free license to record its broadcasts. This offer would mean that CBS would allow Vanderbilt to make and store copies of its news programs and allow persons interested in them to view them on-site at Vanderbilt. It would not, however, allow the Archive to make copies for others or to make compiled tapes. We maintained the position that we had a right to perform these services and not simply keep copies of the original programs on record. Later in the spring of 1972, CBS also offered a royalty-free license to the National Archives, a move which would ultimately figure prominently in the network's conflict with the Vanderbilt Television News Archive.

I was not particularly surprised by the CBS response. I realized that the copyright issue was something that they were going to pressure us about sooner or later, based on comments they had made since the beginning. Mr. Small, the CBS bureau manager in Washington, had discussed this situation several times in our phone conversation during the showing of the Laos tapes in March of 1971. As I had told him then, the Archive did not consider the material copyrighted. Television was a relatively new process and it wasn't specifically covered in the copyright bill, which had been passed to cover written material. We held the basic position that television, once it was telecast to millions of people, came into public domain. Certainly, it was available for study.

In the fall of 1972, the threat of a lawsuit against Vanderbilt over this issue became evident. Jim Pilkington and I spent an hour or so talking with Samuel Suratt, the archivist at CBS, in September, 1972. Suratt said we were costing the network thousands of dollars and indicated that CBS was making the same material available that we were. He discussed with us a market which they hoped to develop to sell videotaped copies of their news programs in large numbers for profit. We felt that they were not really talking about making the material available for review and research. We tried to make our position and reasoning clear, but he refused to recognize or admit the difference between what we were doing and what the network proposed to do. By the end of this meeting, Suratt had stated that CBS didn't want to sue Vanderbilt but that network executives felt they had to take some kind of action.

In the spring of 1972, all three national networks had faced investigation of their operations. Representative Harley Staggers, chairman of the House Commerce Committee and its Special Subcommittee on Investigations, launched an investigation of the entire television industry and scheduled public hearings in May, 1972. The investigation focused partly on the question of whether the networks staged events or depicted faked incidents as real in their news programming. Staff members of the committee visited the Archive twice to look through the tapes we had, and then they asked us to make a compiled tape of some of the items they wanted to examine in the hearings. We were subpoenaed by the Staggers Committee to bring the requested tapes to Washington. In the Book of Rules of the House of Representatives, which was delivered to me with the subpoena, I learned that it was customary for witnesses to submit a written statement in advance, so I prepared and submitted the following statement prior to my appearance at the hearing.

Mr. Chairman, Members of the Subcommittee:

I am here today as a representative of the Television News Archive of Vanderbilt University, located in Nashville, Tennessee. The reason for my appearance is to explain the background and purpose of this Archive which, to the best of my knowledge, is unique. At least until such time as the nature and work of this unique library function becomes better known, we welcome opportunities to make this explanation when materials from the collection are used in public showings.

The Vanderbilt Television News Archive comprises a videotape collection of the evening news broadcasts of the three major television networks dating back to August 5, 1968. The collection has been, and on a daily basis continues to be, built by videotaping these news programs off the air as they are broadcast from the local stations in Nashville. At present the collection consists of approximately 2000 hours of videotaped news broadcasts.

A non-profit enterprise, the Vanderbilt Television News Archive exists for the sole purpose of maintaining the collection for reference and research, in the same manner that collections of printed materials are systematically retained for use through libraries. The material is available for use at the library in Nashville and, on a rental basis only, for use elsewhere. None of the material is sold, and the Archive specifies that it not be duplicated or rebroadcast, either over radio or television.

The Archive does not involve itself in the content of the material beyond such abstracting and indexing procedures as are basic to the use of the collection. Moreover, the Archive is not responsible for opinions and/or judgments respecting this content that might be expressed by those using the material.

To date authors, graduate and undergraduate students, professors, research institutions, television station personnel, and public officials have used the collection. Uses in these categories have increased substantially since publication, in March, of the first number of the TELEVISION NEWS INDEX AND ABSTRACTS, for the month of January, 1972. The February, 1972 number of the index has recently been published and the March and April numbers are in the process of publication.

The Vanderbilt Television News Archive first began to take shape in the minds of a group at Vanderbilt in June of 1968. This group believed that tapes of the newscasts should be preserved for study by present and future scholars. Following a presentation of this need, a committee consisting of the Secretary of the University, the director of the Joint University Libraries—which serves Vanderbilt University and two other educational institutions in Nashville—and professors and department heads of the University was appointed to oversee the development of an experimental project for the taping and retention of the newscasts. At the outset, a three month experimental period was set, covering the period from August 5 to November 5, 1968, to include off-the-air taping both of the newscasts and the two national political conventions, as well as the coverage of the Presidential election itself. In the course of the experiment, determination was made that the project should be continued, which has been done.

The tapes that will be shown today have been rented by the House of Representatives Investigation Subcommittee on the same basis that material would be and has been made available to others at their request.

At the request of this subcommittee, and in accord with our standard charges for services, the Archive put together on one continuous tape various items the subcommittee staff had selected earlier and reviewed on tapes of the full programs. You may notice that some of the tapes carry network, date, and time identifications and that some do not. Camera marking of the tapes with this identification began in January, 1971, when better equipment was secured to make this possible.

Among the materials requested from the Archive by the subcommittee is an hour-long compilation of the coverage of the Democratic National Convention on the evening of Wednesday, August 28, 1968, by one network—NBC. This tape was made during the experimental period of the Archive essentially as an experiment, to determine the feasibility of compiling on one tape or a series of tapes, related items on the same subject for study of the material by subject. Such "subject matter" tapes, it was believed, would greatly facilitate research by those using the Archive.

To prove to ourselves that such electronic compilation was possible, without harm to the master recordings, we undertook to compile a tape in October, 1968. Widespread interest in the dramatic events at the Democratic Convention on the Wednesday evening afore-mentioned, coupled with the fact that the demonstrations, police actions, and comments concerning them could be easily identified and selected, caused us to choose this as the "subject matter" for this compiled tape. The NBC coverage was chosen because that network had, according to the ratings, the largest viewing audience on that particular night. Because of inexperience with the equipment, we did encounter difficulties, which are obvious on the completed tape.

We did, however, satisfy ourselves that such compilations were possible. The tape we made then has been retained in the Archive. A copy was furnished to this committee at your request.

The Vanderbilt Television News Archive is directed by a three-man committee appointed by the Chancellor of Vanderbilt University on authorization of the executive committee of the University's Board of Trust. Chaired by Robert A. McGaw, secretary of the University, the committee includes Frank P. Grisham, director of the Joint University Libraries, and myself as administrative consultant. James P. Pilkington is the administrator of the Archive.

⁕

When I appeared before the committee in Washington on May 17, 1972, I wanted to make clear that the only participation of the Vanderbilt Television News Archive was in making the material available at the request of the Staggers Committee and that we had not selected the items to be shown.

The committee apparently did find some indication of news staging on the part of both CBS and ABC. According to an article in the October 8, 1972, issue of the *Tennessean*, the Federal Communications Commission asked these two networks to respond to certain specific charges which were raised in the hearings.

The Staggers Committee was a good example of what I thought the Archive was for—if someone wanted to review material, there was a way to do because of the tapes we had at the Archive. Another example was the investigation of the Attica State Prison riots, which had occurred in September, 1971. The riots had received significant coverage on the network evening news programs. In March of 1972, I received a call from Frank G. Carrington, executive director of Americans for Effective Law Enforcement, located in

Chicago. Carrington said that he was very interested in the subject of the Attica Prison uprising and would like to visit the Archive to see what materials we had. The New York State Commission appointed to investigate the riots at Attica also asked that we prepare compiled tapes of the network coverage of the riots. Jim Pilkington and I looked through the coverage, made a list of the item involving Attica, and then completed the tapes. These were loaned to the New York State Commission in accordance with our general rules and policies. We understood that these tapes were reviewed by the commission as part of its investigation.

I retired from Metropolitan in May, 1972, so I was then able to devote all of my time to the Archive except for limited duties as mayor of the Nashville satellite city of Oak Hill. In June, Jim Pilkington, Frank Grisham, and I attended the Conference on Electronic Journalism, sponsored by the Herbert Hoover Presidential Library Association and held at the Airlie House, a conference center in Warrenton, Virginia, just outside of Washington, D.C. We had been invited to the conference by John T. McCarty, executive director of the Herbert Hoover Library Association. McCarty had earlier visited the Archive in Nashville. Only a limited number of people had been invited to this conference so that those attending could discuss the issues openly and frankly with one another.

McCarty outlined the three main goals of the conference in his opening statements. The first goal was to examine the question of whether libraries should take a close look at the "electronic journalism" with which the current generation of students had grown up, examine how television news programs were compiled, and consider these programs as library documents which should be made available to students and scholars.

Jim, Frank, and I served on the opening panel to talk about this issue. This conference was perhaps the best public exposure the Archive had received to that date. My statements were intended to explain how the Archive had begun and to emphasize our belief in the importance of television news programs being kept on record. Jim and Frank followed with their presentations, with Jim's focusing specifically on the operations and services provided by the Archive and Frank's examining the value of the collection to research librarians.

The second goal of the conference was to talk about the underground press and the fact that themes developed in the underground press often appear in the conventional media. The third goal was to discuss from all points of view the controversial Fairness Doctrine as to whether or not the first amendment does in fact apply to electronic journalism. [1]

Among those participating in the conference were John Lynch, ABC's Washington bureau chief, and Joseph DeFranco, CBS's legal counsel. Reuven Frank, president of NBC News, was scheduled but was unable to attend because of the terrible weather conditions caused by Hurricane Agnes. Also attending the conference were professors, representatives of smaller broadcasting companies, columnists, critics, and FCC Commissioner Richard E. Wiley. The prepared remarks of all those on the program (including those such as Frank, who didn't actually make it to the conference) were published in a book of proceedings. In that book was also printed a copy of the first brochure for the Vanderbilt Television News Archive, which had only recently been prepared. [See Appendix C for a copy of this brochure.] As we were receiving more and more requests about the Archive, we felt that we needed something that would be easy to mail to tell people about the Archive and answer questions about how to use its services.

Jim and I continued to try to spread the word about the Archive to people and institutions that might be interested in our services. In the fall, we visited with James P. Murphy at the Annenberg School of Communications of the University of Pennsylvania in Philadelphia. We informed him about the purpose and activities of the Archive; in addition, we hoped to establish the foundation for possible future requests for financial assistance.

In the fall of 1972, we also actively participated in another conference to discuss television. At the University of Delaware, Jim and I were invited to a conference sponsored by the National Archives, and we spent several days there.

Freedom of the press is a very complicated issue, particularly when you start talking about television. We started out in this country thinking in terms of freedom for all these little newspapers with limited circulation. It's a very different thing when you're talking about three very powerful television networks.

In the course of this conference, the executive producer of one of the network news programs spoke of television's responsibility for getting the United States out of Vietnam. I know that he expressed this opinion because several people in the audience questioned him as to whether or not television deserved this credit. He insisted that they did deserve such credit.

I was reminded of a story I had seen on the network news one evening. I was watching the news from two networks at the same time on two television sets, as I often did. NBC reported that the South Vietnamese Marines had been going north to a village, and when they passed the villagers who were going south, the villagers would not even speak to them. So, the report said, the South Vietnamese Marines became angry and tore the village apart. However, that same evening, CBS reported a story about the same village. The CBS report indicated that the North Vietnamese shelling had set this village on fire, and when the villagers fled south, the South Vietnamese Marines went in and tore down part of the burning village to try to save the rest. NBC came on the next night and said they had misreported the story because of a breakdown in battlefield communications.

What bothered me most about this incident was that I had to wonder how many times stories had been "misreported" and we never knew about it. I think the only reason we knew about this incident was that it had been reported on CBS on exactly the same day—if CBS had made its report a few days later, I doubt that NBC would have made any mention of it, assuming everyone would have forgotten the report anyway.

I wouldn't have even thought of bringing this up at the meeting where the executive producer spoke, but if I had been in a private conversation with him I would certainly have asked if he thought it was that sort of reporting that helped get the United States out of Vietnam. In addition, I would have asked if he was familiar with the NBC coverage of the Kent State incident (see page 60) and if he believed this kind of reporting also helped get us out of Vietnam.

We had been promised by the National Archives that we would receive a transcript of the conference proceedings. I contacted the National Archives several times before I finally received a copy. When I did receive a copy of the proceedings, there was no mention of the executive producer's statement that television deserved the credit for getting the United States out of Vietnam or other remarks concerning that statement. In hindsight, I wondered if the executive producer had decided that it was not wise to claim this credit because f the network deserved the credit for getting the United States out of Vietnam, some would question whether it also deserved the credit for getting the United States into Vietnam in the first place and for keeping our country involved here as long as it was.

Toward the end of 1972, the Archive enjoyed a visit from staff members of the Hoover Institution, with whom we had kept in touch since my initial visit in 1970. Dennis L. Bark, assistant to Director Dr. Glenn Campbell, wrote to me that Dick Larry had visited the Hoover Institution and had talked at length about our Archive. Dr. Campbell then asked Bark and Brien Benson, head of the publications department, to visit us and familiarize themselves with our operations. We had a very pleasant visit with them and spent the better part of a day showing them our facilities and discussing our activities and services.

In the coming years, Dick Larry would become a very important individual in the continued success of the Archive. We were fortunate to have the support of many people around the country, and in the very near future, we were going to need it. By the end of 1973, our problems with CBS would reach climax.

Chapter Five

Kill The Messenger: CBS Files Suit

Against Vanderbilt For Taping News Programs

F avorable responses to the *Index and Abstracts* led to an increase in requests for services of the Archive. We continued our work on the indexing and data retrieval system, and well over two-thirds of the collection had been abstracted to facilitate the indexing process. This aspect of our work was greatly aided by a grant from the Ford Foundation to index and abstract all the tapes prior to 1972.

Representatives from the Ford Foundation were in Nashville to discuss this grant with us in May of 1973, and they joined us in a meeting with Senator Howard Baker on May 26 to talk about long-term plans for the Television News Archive project. The Ford Foundation also wanted to discuss with Senator Baker their interest and participation in the support of public television. The meeting took place in Senator Baker's hotel suite. Those attending, in addition to Senator Baker and three members of his staff, were Chancellor Alexander Heard, who was at that time also chairman of the Ford Foundation; Fred W. Friendly, advisor on television for the Ford Foundation; Stuart F. Sucherman, program officer for public broadcasting for the Ford Foundation; and me.

Following the meeting, Chancellor Heard wrote to Senator Baker thanking him for his interest and participation.

Senator Baker's interest in and support of our project never wavered from the very early days when I met with him in Washington to tell him about the project. He took every opportunity to talk about the importance of the television news programs being kept as a historical record. Senator Baker had been invited to make some remarks before the National Association of Broadcasters in late March, 1973. He spoke primarily about the need for broadcasters to accept the responsibility for regulating their own programming and said that he was in favor of broadcasting with a minimum of federal regulations. However, Senator Baker also used the occasion to mention the Vanderbilt Television News Archive and to say that he was "appalled that there is no voluntary system for the permanent retention and cataloging of major historical events for posterity." He urged the broadcasting industry to voluntarily assume the task of maintaining and making available copies of their programs as historical documents.

Senator Baker continued his efforts to have the Library of Congress become the permanent repository for copies of news programs, and he reintroduced the bill in September, 1973. He had sent us a draft of the bill earlier, and Chancellor Heard, Bob McGaw, Frank Grisham, Jim Pilkington, Jeff Carr, and I discussed it in some detail. I later met with Ward White, who was minority counsel of the Senate Communications Committee, representing Senator Baker, to outline some of our ideas. I would find myself working more and more closely with White over the next few years as he and Senator Baker became extremely involved in new copyright legislation.

In the days following the May 26 meeting with Senator Baker, Jim Pilkington and Stuart Sucherman worked out the terms of agreement for a grant from the Ford Foundation, and we began receiving funds from them in

June. Funding continued from the Carthage/Scaife Foundations through the grant we had been awarded in 1970, and we hoped to secure additional financing from them in the future, so I tried to keep them fully up-to-date on our plans and activities. Early in 1973, Mrs. Cordelia Scaife May, Richard Scaife's sister, visited us at the Archive; she wrote to me of her visit that it "was one of the most interesting days I've ever spent. I hope you feel satisfaction that you are engaged in work that is both unique and important."

I visited with Dan McMichael of the Carthage/Scaife Foundations in Pittsburgh on June 11, 1973. I summarized the content of our conversation in a memorandum to Chancellor Alexander Heard, a portion of which is shown below.

MEMORANDUM

TO: Chancellor Heard
FROM: Paul Simpson
DATE: June 13, 1973
SUBJECT: Trip to Pittsburgh June 11, 1973

I met with Dan McMichael in the morning. He expressed a strong continuing interest in the Vanderbilt Television News Archive and confidence in its being properly administered by Vanderbilt University through the Administrative Committee. He expressed the hope that the Archive would continue to operate without outside control and with the necessary flexibility so important to a still new interprise (sic). He expressed confidence that the Archive would continue to have as its objective the maintenance of a collection of videotapes of the evening news broadcasts of the major television networks for use, on as open and convenient a bases (sic) as possible, in consideration of costs and technology and that the Archive would continue its policy of refusing to express editorial opinion concerning the material it collects. He feels that the matter of abstracting and indexing the back collection in the same manner as the year 1972 is of utmost importance and expressed his willingness to be of any help possible in this matter. . . . I was encouraged by my visit to feel that the staff and Trustees of the Carthage and Scaife Family Charitable Trusts continue to be very much interested in the future of the Vanderbilt Television News Archive.

Everything seemed to move along quite smoothly for the Archive through the first half of 1973. At a conference held by the National Archives and Record Service, one speaker said, "The boldest and most exciting thing taking place in archival circles today is what those people at Vanderbilt are doing." His quote was used in an article entitled "Preserving the Evening News" in the *Vanderbilt Alumnus*. This article gave a history of the development of the Archive, noting that it had grown "from a table top in the old rare book section to a suite of attractive offices equipped with a viewing area for students and researchers, a room for the technical work, a small conference viewing area, and space for work connected with monthly publication of the *Television News Index and Abstracts*, begun in January, 1972." The article also reported that the Archive's collection had attracted numerous users from throughout the United States and that it was being used for ten different studies of the 1972 Presidential election. Largely because of the *Index and Abstracts*, the Archive was gaining more and more attention on a national level.

As the Archive became more recognized as a unique collection, CBS became more and more concerned about what we were doing. In July, Chancellor Heard received a letter from Val Sanford, a Nashville attorney, writing on behalf of CBS. Sanford's letter made clear that the Vanderbilt Television News Archive should discontinue its "violation of the property rights of CBS" or expect a lawsuit. He stated that beginning in April, 1973, CBS had been registering the "CBS Evening News with Walter Cronkite" with the copyright office and planned to continue such registration. CBS again said it would be willing to consider a royalty-free license to Vanderbilt, with attendant restrictions, as a way to avoid litigation.

Jeff Carr was Vanderbilt's legal officer, and he wrote to Sanford suggesting a meeting to discuss this issue. Jeff, Robert McGaw, Frank Grisham, Jim Pilkington, and I met with Sanford on July 30, 1973, at the Archive's office. At the meeting, Sanford informed us that CBS was registering each news program with the copyright office as a motion picture not reproduced for sale. It was our understanding that under this provision CBS was required to submit to the copyright office prints of only two scenes from each program, not a tape of the full program. Sanford was fairly definite in stating that CBS was determined to pursue litigation if we could not negotiate a license agreement. We were equally definite in indicating that we wished to continue operation of the Archive under its current procedures, which we believed had been carefully designed to avoid infringing the rights of the networks.

Sanford suggested that we propose the terms of a license agreement for consideration, and we later did so, basically stating that the Archive should be able to record the material off the air, abstract and index the programs, and be allowed to make duplicate copies and compiled tapes as necessary for review by those wishing to use the Archive. In his letter outlining these terms, Jeff Carr indicated again that we did not consider the activities of the Archive a violation of CBS's property rights, pointing out that the law concerning copyright of a television news broadcast was not clear.

We were never able to reach any agreement concerning a royalty-free license. CBS appeared to be willing to consider a license for us to record and store tapes of the news programs and to allow anyone to view the tapes on site at the Archive, but we would not be allowed to make copies of the tapes for others or to make compiled tapes from the original programs. We never thought that would work satisfactorily, and we said so. In an October 15, 1973, letter to Jeff Carr, Val Sanford noted that the basic point of disagreement concerned the duplication, compilation, and loan aspects of the Archive's program and that CBS would not consent to such use of its material.

After studying the copyright law and the statute under which CBS was registering its programs, our advisors felt that we had a strong position on the issue. Clearly, we would have preferred *not* to be sued by CBS, but we were prepared should the network decide to file suit.

CBS brought suit against Vanderbilt on December 21, 1973. We heard about the suit in a rather unusual way. It was the last day of work before the Christmas break at Vanderbilt. On that morning, Jim Pilkington and I noticed a television camera crew taking pictures of the front of the library building. We wondered why they were doing this. We found out later, when Jeff Carr got a call from the *New York Times* and I received a call from *Newsday* asking us about the lawsuit CBS had filed against Vanderbilt. The local CBS station ran a news item about it. At that point, we had not been served. It was a dramatic moment in the Archive's history to learn about it that way. In a statement issued by the Vanderbilt press office that evening and quoted in the *New York Times* the following morning, Chancellor Heard stated, "The procedures of the television news archive have been carefully designed in an effort to insure that they do not infringe rights of CBS or of the other networks."

Even though the lawsuit received extensive coverage in the printed press and the local CBS station ran a story about it, the suit was never mentioned on any of the network news programs—by CBS, NBC, or ABC. Even later when the suit was resolved, it was never mentioned by the networks. That treatment reaffirmed my belief that the networks really didn't want to give any publicity to the Vanderbilt Television News Archive or to the fact that tapes of the actual broadcasts were available for review and research.

There was much coverage in the printed press throughout the three years we were defending the lawsuit. Basically, the only real coverage that the Vanderbilt Television News Archive received, other than in the local news media, resulted from the lawsuit. In fact, I wonder if CBS later regretted that it ever brought the lawsuit simply because it led to so much publicity for the Archive. By far, most of the publicity was favorable to Vanderbilt. Perhaps my two favorite news articles from the early days of the lawsuit were those in the *Wall Street Journal* and the *village VOICE* because those two papers cover a broad spectrum of readership. The *Wall Street Journal* article stated, ". . . surely there ought to be some collection of television news, which no doubt has vast and subtle effects on American life. . . . So it seems to us that a disinterested observer can only hope that . . . the courts will somehow arrive at a Solomonic solution that will allay CBS' fears yet will not halt Vanderbilt's unique archival undertaking." The *village VOICE* took a much more acerbic approach to its criticism of CBS and its motives.

Many of the news reports were not highly critical of CBS, but I don't think there were very many people, except the networks, who were ever opposed to what the Archive was doing. Most people thought it was a good thing. Over the course of the lawsuit, Vanderbilt received a significant number of letters of support and encouragement from throughout the country.

Papers were served on Vanderbilt University on January 4, 1974. CBS asked for an injunction to prevent Vanderbilt from continuing the Television News Archive. They also asked that the court order the tapes of the CBS programs which the Archive had be submitted to CBS. This request for the turning over of the tapes led to an interesting statement by the CBS attorney. When asked by the news media what would be done with the tapes if they were given to CBS, he responded that they would probably be erased. CBS received tremendous criticism in the print media because of this statement. I think part of the criticism was caused by the fact that, at the same time, CBS was demanding that Nixon's tapes in the White House be turned over for public scrutiny.

CBS filed interrogatories against us—massive lists of questions which required extensive work to prepare the answers, but we prepared them. Val Sanford, accompanied by a well-known Washington attorney, E. Barrett Prettyman, took a deposition from Jim Pilkington one day and then spent the whole next day taking a deposition from me. I have to admit that I didn't particularly enjoy the day of deposition, but I didn't especially dislike it either. Since I had a legal background and had by that time spent several years studying the networks' news operations and, therefore, knew a great deal about how they operated, the process wasn't difficult for me. They asked a lot of questions and I gave a lot of answers. They returned later and took another deposition from Jim. They didn't ask to take another deposition from me; I guess they thought I had talked enough.

Soon after CBS took our depositions, I went with Jeff Carr and our two lawyers to New York to take depositions of the CBS employees. We deposed the news department people, but we did not depose Walter Cronkite. I never really had any idea of what Cronkite's feeling was about this matter.

I sat in on the depositions, except the lawyers wouldn't let me stay when they started talking about finances. At that point, the CBS attorney asked me go out into the waiting room and I did. I did have an opportunity to suggest to Jeff that he might want to ask the CBS people if any study had ever been made as to whether or not CBS made a profit from its news operation. I did that because I had heard that such a study had been made and that it revealed that CBS did make a profit from its news operation.

Over the course of the legal dispute with CBS, Chancellor Alexander Heard corresponded with Arthur Taylor, president of CBS at that time. In his first letter, February 22, 1974, Taylor outlined the network's position and noted that he was releasing his letter to the press. CBS also released Chancellor Heard's March 5 reply, along with Taylor's follow-up letter. The March 18, 1974, issue of *Broadcasting* outlined some of the contents of this correspondence in an article entitled "CBS, Vanderbilt duel over legal niceties of news archives." The article pointed out Chancellor Heard's reminder to CBS that the Archive did not sell any tapes and that Vanderbilt did not consider the making of compiled tapes "editing," as charged by the network. Taylor, however, insisted that Vanderbilt continued to avoid the central issue—"that Vanderbilt Television News Archive's unauthorized video taping, editing, and distributing of the 'CBS Evening News' . . . constitute an infringement of CBS property rights."

On March 25, 1974, Vanderbilt filed two motions and supporting briefs asking the Court to dismiss the complaint of CBS that the Vanderbilt Television News Archive violated CBS copyrights. As expected, CBS then filed lengthy documents in opposition to our motion to dismiss.

All along, CBS's primary objection was to the making of copies and especially of compiled tapes. I felt that one reason the networks so vehemently opposed the making of compiled tapes was that network executives understood from experience what can happen when items are excerpted and put together on a separate tape. The networks, in effect, make a compiled tape everyday when producers compose their news programs, so they realize there is potential for error and bias. Only a small part of the great amount of material the networks have each day is shown to the American people; no one ever gets to see the complete coverage from which these segments were selected (as I pointed out earlier, during the Westmoreland hearings, the networks risked a contempt of Congress citation by refusing to allow outtakes to be viewed). We continuously pointed out that whenever we made a compiled tape the original complete programs from which the items were taken were available for anyone to review.

We felt that without being able to make copies and compiled tapes, the Archive could not really fulfill its purposes. Many groups who used the Archive agreed. In February, 1974, Accuracy in Media, Inc., published a long review of the conflict between CBS and Vanderbilt in its *AIM Report*. The review was highly supportive of the Archive's work and stated that CBS's proposed agreement to limit the use of the tapes to the premises of Vanderbilt "would destroy the value of the Vanderbilt collection . . . as far as AIM was concerned, since we could not afford to send an analyst to Nashville every time we wanted to find out what CBS had said on a particular news program." The article further stated that "Rather than damage or destroy this valuable public service, CBS should make the university a substantial grant to support the valuable work being done by the Television News Archive." At the annual CBS shareholders meeting, AIM Chairman Reed Irvine presented a resolution calling upon the network to drop its suit. The resolution was hotly debated by Irvine and by CBS Chairman William S. Paley and CBS President Arthur Taylor, who opposed its adoption. The June, 1974, *AIM Report* printed the full text of the debate. Not surprisingly, the resolution failed, but, as the *Report* indicates, AIM picked up a fair amount of support for its position. There were other organizations which attempted to persuade CBS to drop its suit against Vanderbilt because they felt the collection was of significant value to scholars and researchers. The Council on Children, Media, and Merchandising, a Washington-based organization, went so far as to file an Amicus brief with the court in June, supporting Vanderbilt's request to have the suit dismissed. Naturally, CBS filed a request to have this brief disregarded. In any case, Vanderbilt's motion to dismiss was denied.

There were a tremendous number of filings of papers from both sides, and reports in the printed press usually followed. Some of these articles simply reported the facts, but many were clearly favorable to Vanderbilt's position. For example, a column by Patrick Buchanan in the April 6, 1974, *TV Guide* stated that "CBS apprehension is no justification for denying scholars, journalists, and media critics full access to this irreplaceable and priceless slice of recent history." *The Tennessean Magazine* of July 7, 1974, did a lengthy story entitled "The Battle for Walter Cronkite," which outlined both the CBS and Vanderbilt positions.

In April, 1974, CBS announced a three-month, royalty-free license agreement with the National Archives, which would allow the Archives to record CBS News television broadcasts and make copies of the recordings available for use at the sixteen branch Archives and Presidential libraries around the country. This agreement did not allow for making copies of the tapes for use elsewhere or for making compiled tapes. This license was followed, in November, by the announcement of a new two-year agreement between the Archives and CBS which did allow the National Archives to provide copies for use by other libraries in accord with the interlibrary loan code of the American Library Association.

At this point, CBS suggested that Vanderbilt turn over its tapes to the National Archives. We felt that we could not agree to this for several reasons. The agreement covered only two years and there was no guarantee that it would be extended. In addition, it involved only one network (CBS), and we felt that it was important to keep our collection of news broadcasts from the three national networks intact. We also reminded CBS that the ALA interlibrary loan code did not apply to all of those who could make use of the tapes, most notably undergraduate students. The issue of compiled tapes was also very important to us since it represented a considerable savings of effort and money for students and other researchers, and the agreement with the National Archives still did not allow for making compiled tapes.

Around this same time, CBS also announced a policy under which it would license schools and school districts to record its news programs off the air for in-school educational purposes. This policy, however, stipulated that the tapes must be erased after thirty days.

I think CBS worked out these agreements largely to strengthen its position on the copyright debate and the lawsuit because it enabled CBS to say that the network was making the same material available that we were. CBS did often refer to these arrangements when talking about the network's opposition to the Vanderbilt Archive.

At this period of time, there was significant interest in developing some kind of cooperative approach between the broadcasting community and the federal government for preservation of America's television heritage. In March of 1974, I was invited by the American Film Institute to attend a luncheon meeting at the Kennedy Center in Washington to discuss this issue. The invitation made clear that all participants would be responsible for their own expenses except for the cost of the luncheon. About twenty people, including representatives from the Library of Congress, the National Archives, the National Academy of Television Arts and Sciences, and other organizations, attended the March 8 meeting. There was extensive discussion at the meeting about retaining television programs with, it seemed to me, more emphasis on entertainment television than on television news. There also was very little discussion on the question of making such material available for use by scholars and researchers. The meeting ended with a decision that a smaller committee would be appointed from those present to discuss the matter further.

The Archive's primary concern from the beginning had been making the material available to the public, and Vanderbilt maintained its basic position that the material was not copyrighted and was in the public domain, but we had developed our policies for use of the tapes similar to those the library used for print materials. For example, when people go to Vanderbilt's library to check out books, the library doesn't require them to sign a statement that they're not going to violate the copyright of those books. That's their personal responsibility. So that's what we did with the tapes. People who borrowed tapes were responsible for the copyright issue; we were not. At one point, one of the networks wanted us to sign an agreement that we wouldn't let another network borrow any tapes because it might use them. Our answer to that was that the network should sue the other network if they felt they violated the copyright.

Very early on, we had people sign an agreement that they would neither rebroadcast nor duplicate the tapes. Later, after revision of the copyright law, all we did was include a notice that the tape was copyrighted material; it was the borrower's responsibility to use the tape within the copyright laws. Also, the Archive never sold any tapes but simply furnished a copy for use for a limited period of time, with the understanding that the tape would be returned and a fee would be paid for service charges.

A bill for general revision of the 1909 copyright law was pending in Congress in 1974; the bill included several provisions specifically for the copyrighting of television programs, including news programs. When the bill first came to the Senate floor in the fall of 1974, it contained provisions that would have prevented anyone from ever videotaping the television news programs. Senator Howard Baker then proposed what came to be known as the Baker Amendment, or sometimes the Baker-Vanderbilt Amendment, which would permit certain libraries that met conditions similar to Vanderbilt's to do what Vanderbilt was doing in taping the evening news broadcasts and making them available for historical and scholarly research. The amendment was accepted unanimously in the Senate in September, 1974, and added to the bill.

Both the Nashville *Tennessean* and the *Nashville Banner* ran articles reporting the approval of the Baker Amendment in the Senate. The *Nashville Banner* article of September 10, 1974, quoted Senator Baker as saying that in the absence of laws to require the Library of Congress to establish a television archive, "Our only means of preservation of the nightly news on an organized basis which is accessible to all Americans is at the Vanderbilt Television News Archive." Senator Baker continued his efforts to have the television news archive project established at the Library of Congress, but he felt very strongly that there should be a way for Vanderbilt to continue what we were doing until that dream became a reality. However, the new copyright bill, including the Baker Amendment, was not finally approved by Congress in 1974; therefore, it was necessary to start over with the new Congress in 1975.

During both 1974 and 1975, I continued to contact Ward White for help regarding the copyright matter. I also wrote letters in support of the Baker Amendment to the members of the House and the Senate and visited with members of the House Committee and Senate Committee on the same matter. I had by that time learned of the importance of contacting both House and Senate staff members asking for their help. I made numerous trips to Washington working on the copyright bill, all as a private citizen completely at my own expense. I understood that Vanderbilt, as a tax-exempt institution, was not permitted to lobby in Congress. I think the wisdom of this course became completely apparent to me when I called on the single member of the House mark-up committee who brought up the question of my signing a registration in his office as a lobbyist. He was also the only member of the mark-up committee who supported CBS's position regarding the Baker Amendment. I pointed out that I was there as a private citizen at my own expense. I later wondered whether, if I had been there as a lobbyist from Vanderbilt, he would have brought up the matter that Vanderbilt could not lobby without risking its tax-exempt status.

The time and energy required by the lawsuit made it somewhat difficult for the regular work of the Archive to proceed, but everyone made an effort to carry on the work as best we could. We continued taping off the air the regular news broadcasts from all three networks. In addition, during these years, the Archive staff was extremely busy videotaping all of the news coverage and hearings related to Watergate (a brief summary of my opinions regarding Watergate and the media coverage of the incident appears in the final chapter).

In October of 1974, Jim Pilkington talked with Stuart Sucherman of the Ford Foundation about the additional $100,000 promised to the Archive to complete the indexing project, and we did receive the additional funding in early 1975. At the time Jim talked with Sucherman in October, Sucherman indicated that the Ford Foundation was planning to sponsor meetings on the subject of television archiving, to be attended by representatives from the American Film Institute, the Library of Congress, the National Archives, and the three networks. Jim was invited to attend a meeting held at the Ford Foundation on December 19, 1974. Sam Suratt, the CBS archivist, also attended this meeting. A memorandum from Jim about the meeting reported that it concerned primarily entertainment television and indicated that both he and Suratt made an effort to steer away from areas of controversy.

Beginning in February, 1975, CBS changed its legal strategy by using the copyright mark on its *CBS News with Walter Cronkite* program and registering each program as a publication under the existing copyright law, as the copyright revision bill had still not been passed. Also around this time, CBS and Vanderbilt representatives, in an effort to resolve the lawsuit, began regular discussions regarding points of agreement and disagreement.

In the spring of 1975, I went to Washington and met with members and staff of the House Subcommittee on Courts, Civil Liberties, and the Administration of Justice, which was going to hold hearings on the copyright bill and the Baker Amendment. The hearings were scheduled for June. I told them that if anybody wanted to appear against the Baker Amendment, that I wanted to appear in favor of it.

Robert V. Evans, vice-president and general counsel for CBS, appeared at the hearing to speak against the Baker Amendment, and I spoke in support of it on June 12, 1975. Evans stated that the provisions of the Baker Amendment "discriminate unfairly against owners of 'audiovisual news programs' by making their rights inferior to the rights of the owners of other copyrighted works." He also pointed out CBS's agreement with the National Archives and the new CBS policy for licensing school districts to record news programs, saying that because the "problem of access to recordings of news broadcasts is being resolved by private initiative," the amendment was not only discriminatory but unnecessary.

I referred to the National Archives agreement and the CBS school policy in my comments to the subcommittee. The following is a transcript of my remarks made at the hearing. The complete prepared statement, which was entered into the record and is referred to in the remarks below, is printed in Appendix D.

STATEMENT OF MR. PAUL C. SIMPSON
NASHVILLE, TENNESSEE

Mr. Simpson. Mr. Chairman and members of the Subcommittee, I realize that you have an extremely busy schedule today and with your permission I would like to read just part of the statement.

Mr. Kastenmeier. Without objection the remainder of your statement together with the attachment will be accepted as part of the record.

Mr. Simpson. Thank you.

I am Paul Simpson of Nashville, Tennessee, and I am appearing here today as an individual citizen at my own expense. I have, for over seven years now, been interested in the fact that network television news is recognized as the most important source of information about national and international affairs.

I have therefore, believed that it should be retained as broadcast and made as easily and readily available as technology permits, for research, review and study both now and in the future. Since learning in 1968 that these broadcasts were not being retained at the networks or elsewhere, I have devoted a great deal of time to this matter.

In 1968, I was instrumental, financially and otherwise, in the establishment of the Vanderbilt Television News Archive at Vanderbilt University in Nashville, Tennessee. This has been and is the only existing operative archive of video tapes of all three network television evening news programs.

I would like to let the statement speak for itself and make some comments at this time. First of all, about Senator Baker's proposal for the Library of Congress and the reaction of CBS to that proposal. I have been involved in this matter now since the spring of 1968 and when I found that the network programs were not being retained anywhere in the United States, persuaded Vanderbilt University to set up an archives for the purpose of keeping the evening news. I furnished the original relatively small amount of money to start with and that amount of money ran out very shortly. And then I was able to get money from others to continue it.

In January of 1969 I visited all three networks and made an effort to get them to take over the program of retaining the news and making it available. In the spring of 1969, four members of Congress, a Republican Senator from Tennessee, A Republican Congressman from Tennessee, a Democratic Senator from Tennessee, a Democratic Congressman from Tennessee (in the Nashville District) wrote a joint letter to the Library of Congress asking that they look into the question of this material being kept at the Library of Congress.

The Library of Congress sent three people to Nashville to see what the Vanderbilt television news archive was doing and then wrote letters to the presidents of all three networks. I am sorry to say that while two of the networks responded, to the best of my knowledge, the then president of CBS did not acknowledge the first letter from the Library of Congress nor did he acknowledge a follow-up letter written in the fall of that year.

I mention that for one purpose and one purpose only. I think that the urgency of this news material being kept and being made available, both now and in the future, is just too strong to permit it to depend on a network deciding to or not to keep the material or to or not to make it possible for somebody else to; and because I did have experience in '69 to indicate there was not real interest on the part of CBS in the material being kept and being made available.

In regard to the agreement with the National Archives which was made, the final agreement was made last year, I would like to comment briefly on that. The agreement for the National Archives provides that they (CBS) will furnish tapes to the National Archives, that these tapes will be available for viewing at the National Archives, at the branches of the National Archives, or at the Presidential Libraries.

I understand, at the present time, that equipment for viewing the tapes is not available in the branch libraries and I am of the opinion that it is not available at this point in the National Archives. It seems to me, I am sure, that the viewing equipment will be made available but I think it is going to be extremely difficult for a student, a person in Tennessee, to have to go to Atlanta, Georgia and look at a copy of a tape which has been secured by the Georgia office from the National Archives in Washington. I do not think they will have the money to be able to do that.

So far as the interlibrary loan agreement is concerned, the interlibrary loan agreement specifically excludes undergraduate college students. It applies only to graduate students and professors. I think it is absolutely essential that we begin to develop in this country a body of researchers of television and think the only way you can do that is to have college students begin to think about doing it while they are undergraduate students. So, to exclude them I think would be a very bad thing to do.

The agreement also contains a specific provision that the tapes cannot be taken out of the library. Unfortunately, my research over seven years, and this is something I hope will be changed, but my research indicates that almost no libraries at the present time have video tape viewing equipment. On a great many college campuses, the viewing equipment is in a resource learning center which is most often not in the library, most often not controlled by the library. That is something else I personally think should be changed but that is the condition existing now.

So, under the agreement between CBS and the National Archives, the library would not have viewing equipment and the tapes could not be taken, even across campus to another building, to the resource center or to some department that might have video tape viewing equipment. The agreement with the National Archives is limited to a 2 year basis with renewal being negotiated at that time. I think those are some of the faults of the National Archives arrangement.

So far as the school systems are concerned, I have only heard of one school system that has signed up for that, there may be others. I am intrigued by the requirement that the tapes must be erased within 30 days. It would mean, for example, that a professor who wanted to use a tape would certainly have to rush it into his schedule because at the end of 30 days it would have to be erased and he could not use it.

I feel that television news is one of the most important news sources in this country today. Every survey indicates that more people get their knowledge about national and international affairs from the network news programs than they do from any other source. Mr. Taylor, president of CBS, was quoted in Broadcasting Magazine of May 5, 1975, on page 14, when he appeared in the Senate in regard to the Fairness Doctrine, to have said "it is a potential tool for determined and unscrupulous public officials to destroy what is, in effect, the only national daily press that this diverse nation has."

It does not seem proper to me for all of the local presses to be available and then for the only national press not to be available both now and in the future. I am of the opinion that instead of access to it being restricted, I think, as the other two networks apparently think, that it is so important that it should be as widely available as possible.

Thank you, sir.

Mr. Kastenmeier. Mr. Simpson, thank you for your statement. You are not officially associated with Vanderbilt University or Vanderbilt television news archive at Vanderbilt?

Mr. Simpson. The word official is a little bit bothersome to me. I am an unpaid administrative consultant and a member of the three man administrative committee of the archives. My pay is poor but my hours are extremely good.

Mr. Kastenmeier. Mr. Simpson, you are fully familiar nonetheless with the relationship of Vanderbilt University's problem with Columbia Broadcasting System, I take it?

Mr. Simpson. I graduated from law school many years ago and the word fully bothers me; I am not fully informed about everything that takes place. I do know a great deal about it, yes, and I am not trying to dodge the issue, it is just a fact.

Mr. Kastenmeier. I am trying to determine how much of this you are personally familiar with. Are you familiar with the suit, the ongoing suit?

Mr. Simpson. Yes, sir.

Mr. Kastenmeier. It is your understanding that NBC and ABC pose no particular objections to what Vanderbilt University is doing in terms of its news articles?

Mr. Simpson. We understand that is correct. I do not know of my own personal knowledge; I have read accounts stating that to be true.

Mr. Kastenmeier. You stated, however, you received two letters, letters from two networks presumably not the—

Mr. Simpson. I am sorry, I must have misspoken.

Mr. Kastenmeier. —said you or the university had heard from two networks concerning—

Mr. Simpson. The Library of Congress in 1969 wrote all three networks and it did receive word from two.

Mr. Kastenmeier. As far as news programs, do you understand that news program does not include news interview shows and news documentaries and other public affairs presentations?

Mr. Simpson. I would understand it in a term of hard news programs in the way the networks use it. I would also understand it in the same context, the same meaning as "news reporting." In Section 107 of the proposed Copyright Bill which gives to the networks themselves and other news people the right to use copyright material.

Mr. Kastenmeier. There is a substantial difference is there not between an archival use of material and educational use of ephemeral material such as that described by Mr. Evans, that is to say that which is thought to be sold and erased after 30 days as a transitory educational use of material. But when you talk about archival use, you are talking about long term preservation of materials, are you not?

Mr. Simpson. Yes, I think that because of the expenses involved and the present state of technology there are only going to be a very few archives of television news material. I think that will change sometime in the future but now it is going that way so I think whatever archives existed should be available on a national basis and should be as easily available as possible.

Mr. Kastenmeier. The reason I raised that is your description of the use of this collection of Vanderbilt tends to be somewhere between a true archival preservation and an educational use. You talk about it being available to the undergraduates of Vanderbilt in some sort of educational process as opposed to strictly a preservational archival use of material.

Mr. Simpson. I very strongly believe it should be available for both purposes. It is an expensive operation particularly expensive for a library to undertake. We, for example, estimate that only about $2 to $3 out of each $100 of money spent is retrieved in service fees, so it is a very expensive, I think it would be too expensive just to keep it for current years, too expensive just to keep it for use 25 or 50 years from now. So, I think if you can combine the two, that is what should be done.

Mr. Kastenmeier. We have preserved much of motion picture films over the years, although some of the older motion picture films have decayed. Is it your intention that this be preserved over a long period of time, in perpetuity or scholarship uses of those you may wish to examine many, many years hence?

Mr. Simpson. Yes, I think it should be preserved for a long time. And we are somewhat worried by the fact that we do not know how long videotape will last. Definitely the material which Vanderbilt has, which goes back to 1968, should be transferred to archival quality film. It is just the money has not been available to do that.

Mr. Kastenmeier. The gentleman from Massachusetts?

Mr. Drinan. Thank you very much.

I wonder, Mr. Simpson, whether you would say, pursuant to what you say on page 4, that Vanderbilt and every library should have the same rights with regard to CBS news that they have with regard to the *New York Times* and *Atlantic Monthly.*

You say you have traditionally been able to collect and circulate copies of newspapers and other forms of print journalism. I take it you would say there is no difference and that the librarians should have the same rights to both medias?

Mr. Simpson. It seems to me the only difference would be because of what has taken place there should be even more importance in keeping television news than the other—print news.

Mr. Drinan. Aside from the importance, the television you would say has no greater right than the print media as far as copyright?

Mr. Simpson. No, in fact, it seems to me they have less because the television people do have some certain public rights granted to them which newspapers, for example, do not have, such as use of the public airways. I do have figures and I know we do not have time for them, but television is not an unprofitable business and it seems to me that it is not asking too much of them to give up, what in my opinion as a sales manager and a salesman for 38 years, is not a big income, in order to make this material available.

Mr. Drinan. Going back to the practice of CBS in selling the rights to reprint on a photograph, CBS Morning News to various schools; would you think the *New York Times* would have that right or would not have?

Mr. Simpson. I do not know, sir.

I would question very strongly, and this is based on talking with newspaper people over these seven years, I would question very strongly whether or not they would want to exercise a right to sell.

I know you can go into any library in the country, and I checked with the Library of Congress yesterday, you can go in and make copies of excerpts from newspapers. I think we would consider that the *New York Times* was very unavailable if there were only one copy of the microfilm of the *New York Times* in one place in the United States.

Mr. Drinan. On page 2 of your testimony, I am not certain that the electronic media are granted exceptional privileges under the bill. You suggest that under the proposed bill that Section 107 gives special privileges to the electronic media. I think that goes for all the media, does it not?

Mr. Simpson. That is correct. Yes, sir.

Also, may I correct an error or page 2 which I intended to correct when I started. The bottom of the page says required "by law" to air newsbroadcasts. "By law" is not correct. There is no law I understand but as a matter of practice of the FCC, any local television station that had no news program would have an extremely difficult time in getting their license renewed.

Mr. Drinan. Are you completely satisfied for your purposes with H.R.2223 or would we have to also add the bill of Senator Baker?

Mr. Simpson. I am just interested so far as the pending bill is concerned that it not prohibit news archiving and library activity. I am very much of the opinion that there should be a national archives.

Mr. Drinan. Is Senator Baker's bill necessary in addition to this bill to carry out all your purposes?

Mr. Simpson. I suspect that some sort of national funding is necessary. They have had some difficulty at Vanderbilt in raising the funds to keep it operating. I think it should be on a guaranteed basis.

Mr. Drinan. Aside from the funding, sir, for copyright purposes must we add Senator Baker's bill to H.R.2223.

Mr. Simpson. I do not think so for copyright.

Mr. Drinan. Thank you very much.

Mr. Kastenmeier. I just have one or two questions left.

Subsection 4 says a limited number of copies. How many copies did you have in mind. Might there be the necessity of a number of copies.

Mr. Simpson. I do not know. I might say this, I agree very strongly with the theory that there should be no commercial competition with the networks and I suppose that the reason for putting any limited number of copies would be that you want to emphasize that point.

The Vanderbilt television news archive procedures contain a provision, for example, that the material cannot be duplicated or rebroadcast and that is signed before anybody rents the material.

Mr. Kastenmeier. My second question is, and my first question was directed to see whether again we were talking about archival use or educational use. Educational use, you might need a number of copies, archival use you would not need so many copies.

My last question is, to your knowledge, is Vanderbilt the only entity other than potentially the Library of Congress which is presently engaging in this practice?

Mr. Simpson. Yes, sir, it is and the National Archives.

Mr. Kastenmeier. Are there any other universities or other institutions public or semi-public, that have an interest in the use to which you have directed yourself in Vanderbilt?

Mr. Simpson. Yes, the Vanderbilt archives has received requests from all over the world for this information. The monthly index and abstracts published at Vanderbilt University are being distributed to about seven or eight foreign countries by request; and also to approximately 450, mainly libraries in this country.

The point is, Mr. Chairman, that this material is so expensive, just the cost of the raw tape, for example, that it almost has to be for the present time available in one or two locations; but available to other locations through copies of the tapes on a rental basis or through the request of a compiled tape on certain selected cases that they have picked out, they want to see.

Mr. Kastenmeier. Thank you, Mr. Simpson.

I remember that one of the Congressmen at the hearings who was supporting CBS's position raised the question of who was going to be using the tapes because they were afraid somebody might use the material for some purpose they shouldn't. In other words, CBS should be able to show the material to the American people but then restrict what the American people could do with it after they'd seen it.

I continued talking with a number of people about the bill and the Baker Amendment. When the amendment again came before House subcommittee hearings in October, I wrote a letter to Robert Kastenmeier to restate my support for the amendment and the reasons for my support.

Later, the bill went to a conference committee to settle some differences between the Senate and the House. I contacted the staff members and the Congressional members involved in the conference committee work. I made particular effort to see that the history of the legislative activity in both the House and Senate, and in the conference committee, did not adversely affect the Baker Amendment.

Through the work of the conference committee, a minor revision was made to the Baker Amendment, but it did not affect the Vanderbilt Archive project in any way. The revised amendment was included in the new copyright bill when it was eventually passed and signed into law in October of 1976. The Vanderbilt Television News Archive was cited by named example to maintain the legal right of libraries to record and maintain collections of television news.

The CBS lawsuit was still hanging over the Archive at this time, but everyone knew that passage of the copyright bill with the Baker Amendment would affect the lawsuit. We never had any kind of court appearance or any court decision. We didn't push for a court decision and CBS didn't push it to a decision. In December, 1976, attorneys for both CBS and Vanderbilt requested that the suit be dismissed without prejudice. A December 18, 1976, article in the *Nashville Banner* reported the CBS-Vanderbilt agreement to request dismissal and referred to CBS's local attorney Val Sanford in stating that "the recently approved revised copyright laws stipulate, according to Sanford, that although the copyright is valid, libraries and archives, such as Vanderbilt's, may tape the programs." The article noted that the new copyright law would not become effective until 1978, but that Vanderbilt's taping would continue, as it had throughout the years of the lawsuit.

Today, all of the network news programs are copyrighted under provisions of the revised copyright law, but because of the Baker Amendment, what Vanderbilt was and is doing is one of the few things specifically permitted. I think it was clear that the reason Senator Baker introduced the amendment was to allow the Vanderbilt Television News Archive to continue. If the Archive had not existed, I don't think he would ever have introduced the amendment which made it possible for television news programs to be videotaped and kept for posterity. I think this reason alone fully justifies the Archive's establishment and existence.

The outcome of the CBS lawsuit was really more a matter of what happened with the copyright law than of what happened in the court system. Defending the lawsuit had taken a tremendous amount of time and energy over the course of three years. In a memorandum to the full Television News Archive Committee in December of 1975, Robert McGaw had written of the Archive, ". . . operating procedures have not changed significantly since CBS brought suit two years ago. This is not necessarily good; the unhappy truth is that defending the suit absorbs time and money that might have been spent improving the services."

There were, however, a few major events in the history of the Archive during this period which were not directly connected with the lawsuit. One of these was the hiring of John Lynch, who came to the Archive part-time to work on indexing and abstracting in 1975. He was hired full-time six months later and eventually became director of the Archive. This was a highly fortunate appointment, as John contributed significantly to the continued success of the Archive over the years. I continued to be aware of the impact of network television news on American society. In particular, I believed that network news was having increasing impact on national elections, so I wrote the following document to express an idea which I thought would not only serve the national interest but also increase the use and value of the Vanderbilt Television News Archive.

REFLECTIONS ON
1976 ELECTIONS AND T.V. NEWS

Of major importance in 1976 is the national election including primaries—both Democratic and Republican. Because of the campaign spending law especially, but also because it probably will be more difficult to raise large sums for campaigning (even if the new law is held unconstitutional), news, with special emphasis on national television news, will be of primary importance in the campaign. No equal time rules apply to T.V. News, therefore, it will be critical to success or failure as to how issues and candidates are presented on T.V. national news. It will be more difficult to buy T.V. time. There is also beginning to develop a recognition of this fact and also a recognition of the tremendous impact and influence of national T.V.

Since syndicated columnists are a standard part of newspapers and since they cover items of national interest what could be of more national interest in 1976 than how the single most important issue (which will involve discussion of all other issues) the national elections are handled by the most powerful establishment in the country, the T.V. Networks and particularly network news. It seems to me, therefore, that a continuing report, weekly or even more often, on the national elections, with most emphasis on how the national elections are covered by T.V. would be of interest to all newspapers. The T.V. networks have learned that you secure and keep T.V. audiences by featuring conflict and controversy. You show a "battle" between opposing people, institutions and ideas. I would think therefore, that two opposing columnists or commentators would be most likely to create an interested audience. The existence of an interested audience will cause the newspapers and magazines to desire the columns.

It seems to me also, that a 5 minute a week, or bi-weekly, taped discussion between these two opposing columnists on how Network T.V. covered the election that week or on a related item should be of interest to local T.V. stations as part of their news programs. (I do not believe the networks would consider it.) Local T.V. stations buy syndicated entertainment shows–local newspapers buy syndicated national columnists. Why should not local T.V. stations begin to buy syndicated national T.V. commentators on news subjects? Why do not national columnists syndicators begin to work into this market in 1976 in this manner?

I believe two men should be approached on this matter. It seems to me that a national syndication outfit could do this on a strictly commercial basis. The two men should spend at least 3 or 4 days a week at Nashville viewing tapes of the week, or prior week of news. They could request completion of compiled tapes of items which particularly interested them. These two men should devote at least 80 to 90% of their time to this matter. In addition to writing a weekly or twice a week column, they should have the opportunity of writing more lengthy articles and should be prepared at the end of the election in Nov. 1976 to immediately devote full time in writing a lengthy article or book on what they had observed from a years study of T.V. news election coverage as done at the Vanderbilt T.V. News Archive. Their continuing stories could be datelined Nashville, Tennessee. We have in Nashville very fine facilities for taping shows (this is already being done here). They could therefore, tape here in Nashville their shows for syndication to local T.V. stations. The two men could also compare T.V. coverage of the elections with newspaper and news magazine coverage. All of this material is available on the same floor of the library at Vanderbilt as the T.V. News Archive.

I immediately think of Pat Buchanan as a very fine choice for one of the two columnists. I do not think as quickly of the other man but believe he should be someone like Buchanan but with as clear connection to the other party and other side as Buchanan has to his party and his side. He would also hopefully be as well known or better known than Buchanan.

Fred Friendly in his book *Due to Circumstances Beyond Our Control,* published in 1967, stated on the first page that when he and Ed Murrow switched from radio to T.V. ". . . but for the most part we were, as Ed said, just a bunch of old radio hands learning the hard way that cameras need something more than emulsion and light valves to create electronic journalism. *The missing ingredients were conviction, controversy, and a point of view.* " (emphasis added)

The two selected men need to have convictions and a point of view. The controversy furnished by these two opposing convictions and points of view will furnish the market for these reports and the existence of the market will make it relatively easy to persuade newspapers, magazines, and T.V. stations to buy it. Were I in the syndication business, I know I could sell this.

If it is impossible to interest some newspaper chain or syndication concern in this matter, perhaps the remaining part of the Coors T.V. news company would be interested in undertaking this commercial venture.

If neither of the above works out then I think consideration should be given to funding a nationally known and recognized scholar to spend the year at Vanderbilt devoting 90% of his time to reviewing and studying network T.V. coverage of the 1976 election. Perhaps he could do this by also reviewing the "so-called" national newspapers and magazines coverage of the same incidents. He could write weekly and monthly reports which could be offered to newspapers and magazines and then write a full report at the end of the election.

The individual might do a more scholarly job but his study would simply not receive the attention nor secure the audience that the two men would produce. Ideally you would have both. Perhaps you could have both if the two men would pay their own way as a profitable syndication effort. (I think they would).

Just as newspaper columnists write their columns fairly from their point of view, each of the two men selected should be expected and encouraged to do the same. However, men should be selected who would not use this as an opportunity to curry favor with the networks hoping to secure network exposure or positions. They should be unafraid of network or anyone else's displeasure so long as their careful research at the Archive enabled them to back up their conclusions.

All of the above should apply to the scholar who would in addition be expected to be objective as to various points of view and parties.

As I said, my interest in this endeavor was two-fold—I truly felt that it would be in the national interest, and I also knew that it would lead to an increased usage of the valuable collection at the Archive. Unfortunately, nothing ever came of this idea, and I regret somewhat that I did not pursue it more vigorously.

Naturally, the Archive taped all of the 1976 election coverage, including the Democratic and Republican conventions, as it had been doing since August of 1968.

After several years of off-the-air taping and making duplicates and compiled tapes, our one-inch Ampex recording equipment was beginning to wear, and we knew that we probably could not afford expensive new one-inch equipment. We began considering setting up a new off-the-air recording system using 3/4 inch equipment and taping each program in color. We also hoped to eventually make 3/4 inch copies of all the programs we had been taping since 1968 and store the originals for safekeeping. I knew it would take some time to make this idea a reality, so I began talking with people about this matter in the fall of 1976. Some of my fund-raising efforts over the next couple of years would be directly related to securing funds for this purpose.

The three years from December 21, 1973, when CBS filed the lawsuit against Vanderbilt, to December 20, 1976, when the suit was dismissed, were the most trying times we had faced in the Archive's history. It was a difficult three years for all of us involved with the Archive, but we never lost our determination to see that the Archive continued to fulfill the purpose for which it had been established—to see that the national network news programs were preserved and made widely available for study by the American people.

Chapter Six

The Media Elite:

What Have They Done To Our Country?

B ecause of the time required by the lawsuit, as well as the great amount of time I had spent working on the copyright revision bill, fundraising efforts for the Archive had suffered during 1973-1976. We were fortunate that we had secured support from the Ford Foundation early in 1973, and we had the continuing support of the Carthage/Scaife Family Trusts and the Massey and Potter Foundations. We also during these years received grants from the Adolph Coors Foundation and the *Columbus Dispatch.*

Fundraising was a top priority for the Archive for several years following the resolution of the lawsuit. We began a much broader and more intense fund-raising campaign, which had to be more carefully coordinated through Vanderbilt University to be sure we were not working at cross-purposes with the University's overall fundraising. We began keeping in close touch with the fund-raising officers at Vanderbilt regarding solicitations in progress. Financing the activities of the Archive was always a major consideration since we depended on separate contributions to Vanderbilt for the specific purpose of the Archive.

I continued to contact people in numerous funding organizations about money for the Archive. One of these was the Earheart Foundation; we did receive money from the Earheart Foundation and from the Ford Foundation to begin taping the news broadcasts in color on new 3/4 inch cassette equipment. We were glad to switch to cassettes from reel-to-reel tape because we knew there was much less chance of the tapes being damaged in cassette form and also because it was less expensive and in color. We talked for some time about whether to use 1/2 inch cassettes or 3/4 inch. At that time, the 1/2 inch had not reached the stage of reliability that it later has; therefore, we eventually decided on the 3/4 inch. We relied on Ron Moulton's experience in these matters because he had knowledge of technical developments. The Archive was very fortunate to have him because he was interested enough to keep up-to-date. We never made any kind of equipment or technical decision without Ron's advice. Ron knew the use that we intended for the tapes—such as making copies, making compilations, and so forth—and at that time he felt that the 3/4 inch tapes provided the strength and reliability that we needed. Ron was also instrumental in helping locate some used one-inch equipment, which would serve until the new system was ready.

In addition to taping current and future programs on cassette, we wanted to transfer all of the material we already had, beginning with August, 1968, from reel-to-reel to cassette. By 1977, we had more than 4,500 hours of tapes of the network news broadcasts. We started working on a grant application to the National Endowment for the Humanities for funds to duplicate this collection in two copies on 3/4 inch cassette.

In the section of the grant application regarding the significance of the project, Jim Pilkington included some comments that he had made to me many times. Jim frequently expressed his opinion that the mid-1800s would always be more easily researched than the mid-1900s. Printed news material, the major influence in the mid-1800s, was widely available, whereas network television news, the major influence in the mid-1900s, was not available for research and study prior to 1968 when the Vanderbilt Television News Archive started. For example, the development of the Civil Rights issue in the United States can never be fully researched because the major influence on this development (network television news) up to August of 1968 is not available for study.

A somewhat ironic reminder of the importance of retaining this significant part of our nation's history came in a letter from a CBS researcher in June, 1977. The researcher thanks Jim for sending the requested tapes and says, "If it weren't for your Archive, these CBS broadcasts would be lost not only to the world, but especially to CBS. Thanks for saving us." Over the next few years, we also received letters from news department staff members at both ABC and NBC praising the Archive for its services.

We ultimately did receive a matching grant from NEH to make cassette copies of the collection. One of the conditions was that we would store one copy of the tapes somewhere other than at the Archive, so that if something happened at the Archive, there would be a tape elsewhere. We considered a number of places for this storage and eventually began sending a copy of each tape to the Library of Congress, which seemed like the most reasonable place for the tapes to be kept. I was glad about this decision, because I would sometimes wake up in the middle of the night and think about the fact that if anything happened at the Vanderbilt Library, all those tapes would be gone and there would be no way to replace them.

As I mentioned earlier, we continued to receive funding from the Scaife Foundation; several people connected with the Foundation, including Dan McMichael, Dick Larry, and Clyde H. (Terry) Slease, who was Richard Scaife's personal attorney, greatly assisted our activities. All of these men visited the Archive at one time or another over the years and remained highly supportive of the work there.

In 1977, the Scaife Foundation also made a substantial grant to George Washington University for the establishment of a Television News Study Center at the Gelman Library, which would make more available to those in the Washington, D. C., area all of the resources of the Vanderbilt Television News Archive. I think the Scaife Foundation felt that there should be a location in Washington where members of Congress, members of the administration, and others could view tapes of the news programs. In addition, this center would provide for taping of the weekend newscasts, which were not available off-the-air in Nashville at that time.

We did not consider this center to be in competition with us. The people who wrote the grant clearly intended it to be a service center for the use and promotion of the Vanderbilt Archive, and the press release announcing the grant as well as the center's brochure communicated this objective. I really considered the Scaife funding of the center as a further indication of their interest in the Vanderbilt Television News Archive. I think Scaife wanted to help increase the value of the Archive by increasing its use in the Washington area.

The center at George Washington University opened in January, 1979, with a very capable director, Fay Schreibman, with whom I had the pleasure of visiting on several occasions. I thought the center was doing an excellent job, but it unfortunately remained in operation for only a few years. The library did, however, continue to provide equipment for those researchers in the Washington, D. C., area to view tapes from the Vanderbilt Archive. It also continued to tape off the air the weekend programs which were not aired in Nashville.

On one of my visits to the George Washington University Center, I attended a class on television news that was being conducted weekly. I sat in the back row and attended as an observer only. At one point, the person conducting the meeting stated that he thought people acquired their information as much from talking with their friends and associates as they did from television. Fortunately, I was able to keep quiet and not ask the question I would like to have asked: "Who did their friends and associates get their news from before they passed it on?" I still feel that it would have been a good question anywhere except Washington, D. C. It might not have been as good a question there as it would in the rest of the United States, since both the networks and their "friends and associates" could have obtained their news from the *Washington Post*, as the networks relied heavily on this source.

The new Copyright Law, which went into effect in January of 1978, provided for the establishment of an American Television and Radio Archive in the Library of Congress; we kept in touch with them about their plans. In May, 1978, Alexander Heard met with Daniel Boorstin, the librarian of Congress, and others to talk about these plans and about the Vanderbilt Archive. We were still trying to arrange for the Library of Congress to take over what we were doing at Vanderbilt. Boorstin and others at this meeting emphasized that they currently had more materials than they could store, catalog, or handle and that they wanted to see Vanderbilt continue what we were doing. The Library of Congress did not plan to take any news broadcasts off the air. Therefore, Chancellor Heard talked with them in particular about how the Library of Congress might contribute to the financial support of the Vanderbilt Archive. His memorandum regarding the meeting indicates that he suggested some of the difficulty with raising private donations to continue our work. A variety of ideas were discussed, and these discussions continued throughout the next few years.

On August 5, 1978, the Vanderbilt Television News Archive was ten years old. It was a real surprise to me to realize that the Archive had been in existence for a decade. After all, ten years is a relatively long time for something that was started as a three-month experimental project. I was very pleased that we'd made it through ten years, and I felt that the Archive was on a rather sound basis—we had proven that we could make and loan taped copies of the news programs at a reasonable cost. In addition, I felt even more strongly than I had in 1968 that the Archive was needed. So, even though we were having some financial difficulties, I felt that the money would come. There had been enough interest and support over the years to make me feel that way.

My thoughts at the ten-year anniversary of the Archive are perhaps reflected best in a letter I wrote to Sam Fleming, then president of the Board of Trust of Vanderbilt University. Fleming and I were long-time friends. Following a Board of Trust meeting in October of 1978, Sam wrote to me about a report on the Archive which had been made at the meeting, and I wrote the following letter in response.

November 10, 1978

Mr. Sam M. Fleming
President
The Board of Trust of Vanderbilt University
Third National Bank Building
Nashville, Tennessee 37219

Dear Sam:

Thank you for your letter of October 30. I am
sorry that a long standing commitment made several
months before I knew about the Board of Trust meeting
prevented me from attending. I also felt that Bob
McGaw and Jim Pilkington could and would very well
carry out the purpose at the Board of Trust meeting,
which was, I understood, to explain the Television News
Archive and how it operated.

In thinking back over the almost eleven years since
I first visited the news departments of the networks in
the spring of 1968, it seems to me that it has been
almost as though fate had decided that there should be
a television news archive and that it should be successful.
The following facts encourage me to think in this
direction:

The fact that Frank Grisham was at the Joint University
Libraries in the spring of 1968 and was interested and
receptive to the idea when I first approached him. My
subsequent experiences have convinced me that a vast
majority of librarians would not have been interested
and would not have seen the possibilities in 1968.

The fact that Bob McGaw became interested immediately, saw the possibilities, and had the ability to help make the possibility a reality.

The fact that Alexander Heard was Chancellor of Vanderbilt University, saw the possibilities, and was willing for Vanderbilt to undertake the project.

The fact that Jack Massey and Pat Wilson lived in Nashville and were farsighted and generous enough to make the archive financially possible.

The fact that in 1970 Dick Scaife and his associates became interested and have continued to be interested, making the growth of the archive financially possible.

The fact that Jim Pilkington joined the archive in 1971 as Administrator and has accomplished what very few, if any, individuals in the country could have accomplished.

The fact that Senator Howard Baker was a Tennessee Senator, a person of influence in the Congress, and became interested and has continued to be interested.

The fact that Jeff Carr was available when CBS brought the lawsuit. He worked very hard and very effectively during this lawsuit, being fully supported by Vanderbilt—something that most universities probably would not have done.

All of the above, plus the fact that you became interested early, have continued to be interested, and have continuously occupied a position of responsibility at Vanderbilt have made possible the success you so generously referred to in your letter and, I understand, at the Board of Trust meeting.

Again thanks very much for your letter, for your remarks to the Board of Trust meeting, and for your support over the past years.

Sincerely yours,

Paul C. Simpson
Administrative Consultant

As I said, I felt that continued funding would come because of the interest that had been shown in our work. In January of 1979, Vanderbilt secured a pledge from Time, Incorporated for $50,000 to be paid over a five-year period. This support, combined with the NEH grant and funding from the other foundations with which we were working at the time, allowed me to rest a little easier about the Archive's financial situation in 1979.

During 1978 and 1979, I was able to attend a number of conferences around the country dealing with television. One of these was the Media '78 Colorado Conference, held in Denver in December of 1978 and sponsored largely by the Foundation for American Communications. This interesting meeting stressed news coverage of business and industry. Chuck Rossi, with whom I had correspondence and a number of conversations regarding the importance of knowledgeable news coverage of business affairs, was the person at the foundation with whom I had the most contact, both in Denver and at another conference in California. The foundation later ran a short article about the Archive in its newsletter to let business people know about the services we could provide. In March, 1979, I attended the Conference on Off-Air Taping for Educational Uses, held in Washington, D. C., and sponsored by the Subcommittee on Courts, Civil Liberties and the Administration of Justice and the Copyright Office of the Library of Congress. This conference was attended by representatives from the three networks, as well as by representatives from public broadcasting, educational institutions, and archives.

I also began developing some further thoughts about the impact of the national network news. I later put these thoughts together in the following document.

OBSERVATIONS CONCERNING NATIONAL NETWORK TELEVISION NEWS PROGRAMS

March 6, 1980

These observations are intended to supplement those written on July 17, 1968 and June 2, 1969 in the hope that the critical situation outlined in these observations will be considered now. [1]

As pointed out in June, 1969, a former president of a network news department indicated that "conviction, controversy and a point of view" were essential to a successful (presumably in terms of audience secured) news show. This has proven to be eminently correct and has resulted in "controversy" being a very important

---

[1] See pages 15-20 and 32-43 for copies of these earlier "Observations."

and sought after part of all television news. Perhaps this explains why our country has been torn apart by controversy and why it becomes increasingly difficult for any Administration or Congress (Democratic or Republican) to govern the country.

In the 1970s it also became standard for news media, especially electronic, to indicate, at least, that their proper relationship with the United States government was that of an "adversary."

Webster's New World Dictionary defines adversary as "a person who opposes or fights against another; opponent; enemy."

Perhaps our country can survive if domestic and internal matters are reported to the people of the United States by a powerful news medium which emphasizes controversy and prides itself on being an "adversary" to our government.

We are now, however, well into a worldwide situation different from that ever faced before. Satellites have made possible and will expand even more the availability of worldwide instant communication.

There is no question that the United States has very powerful enemies in the world. Communications and their use have become and will become even more a vital part of this conflict. It is better for this conflict to turn on communications than on war.

We would not think of facing a military conflict with our Army, Navy, and Air Force controlled by people or forces that emphasize controversy with our government and consider themselves as "adversaries" to the government. Can we accept without consideration a situation that results in our worldwide communications being controlled by persons and forces who emphasize controversy and state their position is that of an "adversary" to the United States Government.

There is no question that almost without exception our world enemies understand the power of communications and consider control of the means of communications as important as control of their army, navy, and air force. Whenever a change in government takes place almost anywhere in the world, particularly by coup or revolution, the first step of the new government is to take control of the news media.

It seems to me that there must be some middle ground between government control of the news media and control of the media by those who emphasize controversy and proudly consider themselves "adversaries" to the government.

Since the United States came into existence, we have had weapons and powerful explosives controlled by our military forces. We did not consider it necessary to require that these explosives be placed under the President's sole control. When atom and hydrogen bombs were developed, however, we did not take the position that these were just other weapons, other explosives. We rightly said that they were not, that they were so much more powerful that they deserved great consideration and new "rules." We, therefore, considered and then established those rules.

When television came in there was a tendency to treat it as "just another news medium." Insufficient consideration was given to the new "rules" for this new form of communications in view of its great impact. The impact of newspapers and magazines and the impact of television news (see observations of June, 1969) differ as greatly as those of conventional explosives and the nuclear bombs.

With respect to television, we are now proceeding, with the development of satellites, into a completely new situation. There has never been a time, and probably never will be a time, when any print medium will have the ability to go worldwide. Pictures, however, can be seen and understood anywhere; there is no language barrier.

Are we going to make the mistake of treating this entirely new situation by the "old rules," or are we going to say as we did when the nuclear bombs were developed that we must consider and adopt "new rules?"

I very strongly believe that the existence of the United States depends on our giving careful consideration to the questions raised in these observations. I am convinced that I know the "questions." I am sorry to say that I am not convinced that I know the "answers." I am convinced that the answers must be aggressively sought and by as many people as possible and as soon as possible.

When these "Observations" were written, it was my intention to send them to business, political, and news media leaders throughout the United States. For various reasons, the "Observations" were distributed to only a limited number of people in 1980. However, in 1986, I widely distributed the document with the following cover letter, on my personal stationery and at my own expense.

January 10, 1986

Dear :

"The missing ingredients were conviction, controversy and a point of view." This statement is discussed in the enclosed Observations Concerning National Network Television News Programs; written on March 6, 1980 with the intention of distributing them in order to get this matter on the agenda for national discussion. For various reasons they were not distributed then. In recent years there has been an almost complete absence of statements by the news media that its proper relationship with the Government is that of an adversary. [2]

According to recent news items, Dan Rather and CBS are negotiating with television in France to have the "CBS Evening News with Dan Rather" telecast in France the next morning. This indicates (along with arrangements already in effect in other countries)—that the situation referred to in the enclosed material is at hand.

The report of a survey completed in 1980 reveals that the people responsible for news content of the major national news media, including TV networks, have different opinions in many cases from people generally and the Government in certain foreign policy matters.

---

[2] While the national news media apparently decided that it was not smart to continuously refer to their proper position in regard to the government as being that of an adversary, they discontinued using that label but continued to act that way. (Author's comment, 1995)

Does this mean that "conviction" and "a point of view" must be considered as well as "controversy"?

It is also important to remember that in most of the world today television is Government controlled. The people of these countries understand that. Will it, therefore, be difficult, if not impossible, for them to understand that television in the United States is not only NOT Government controlled, but is in fact controlled by people who want to feature "controversy" and have "convictions" and "a point of view" different from the U. S. Government?

T.V. critic Tom Shales of The Washington Post in The Tennessean of 11/18/85 column "Networks vie for summit audience" says "But network news is largely the science of excess, and Americans have learned to live with it." Will foreign audiences understand this "science of excess"?

It is hoped that you will help to get this matter on the agenda for national discussion so that the correct "answers" can be found for the "questions" raised in this letter and the observations of 1980.

Sincerely yours,

Paul C. Simpson

P.S. A copy of the observations of 1968 and/or 1969 will be sent on request.

This letter and the "Observations" were sent to over two hundred leaders throughout the United States. I felt it imperative that this situation be considered and that new rules for broadcast journalism be considered. I heard from a number of people to whom I had sent these letters, but unfortunately nothing was done in the way of a discussion on a national basis. This national discussion had been my desire.

In 1980, Chancellor Heard was continuing his discussions with the Library of Congress about taking over the Archive project or at least becoming associated with it in some way that would give the Archive some long-range security. In addition, Fred Friendly, at Chancellor Heard's request, held discussions with the assistant librarian for research services at the Library of Congress about this matter. Friendly was also very helpful in writing a letter to the William and Flora Hewlett Foundation explaining the discussions with the Library of Congress and the need for short-term funding to keep the Vanderbilt Archive going until some long-range plans could be finalized. We did later receive a two-year grant from the Hewlett Foundation to help in converting our collection of reel-to-reel tapes to cassette format. We also around this time received some funding from the Glenmeade Trust (for the Pew Memorial Trust).

All of us would have liked to remove the need for continuously working on fund-raising; in 1980 we began talking with the John D. and Catherine T. MacArthur Foundation about an endowment. We requested an endowment from MacArthur of $5 million, which would give us around $275,000 a year for operations, allowing us to expand our services a bit. This was the closest we ever came to getting an endowment, but it unfortunately did not come about.

Also in 1980, we started working toward establishing a National Advisory Board for the Archive, recognizing that the Archive must view itself as a national —and even international—service organization. I wrote a proposal [Appendix E] to outline the need for such a National Board and plans for its establishment. This National Board did not actually become a reality for several years.

We also continued seeking financial assistance from the networks, as we had since the beginning. Chancellor Heard spent some time working with Everett Ehrlich of ABC to see about getting financial support for the Archive from all three networks. Ehrlich was very supportive and helpful in contacting the other two networks, but we were again unsuccessful in our efforts.

Our relationship with the networks in the years following the CBS lawsuit resolution remained relatively cordial, and as I've said earlier, we received a number of positive comments from staff members of the networks. However, in July of 1981, we had a minor run-in with NBC, when they objected to the loaning of a tape to PBS which was later used for the program, "Inside Story." NBC's lawyer wrote to us indicating that they strongly objected to the Archive loaning a tape for use in another broadcast. We also later had a similar objection from CBS, when ABC borrowed a tape which was used in a broadcast. After studying the new Copyright Law, our position was that the law intended for the television news archive collection to be available to the general public and that any improper use of loaned material was the responsibility of the user, not the Archive. Jeff Carr corresponded with NBC about this matter for some time, but it did not cause any long-term difficulties for the Archive or, presumably, for NBC. All three of the major networks, as well as PBS, from time to time borrowed tapes of the other networks from the Archive.

Much of my time continued to be spent in fund-raising activities. I contacted numerous individuals and organizations to explain the services we were providing and the need for financial support to continue and possibly expand these services. During this period I received very valuable assistance from Ambassador Joe Rodgers, a Nashvillian. He wrote several letters of introduction for me to various people throughout the United States. This action was very helpful in receiving some additional financial assistance.

During 1982, I did have an opportunity to participate in some activities that were not directly related to fund-raising. I made a presentation at a program entitled "A Seminar on Freedom and Mass Communication," sponsored by the Freedom Foundation at Valley Forge, Pennsylvania, in July of 1982. I showed some tapes and talked about our work at the Archive. Those attending the seminar were primarily teachers; I also spoke briefly about how news programs are put together and some of the things they should encourage their students to think about when watching the network news. I later spoke at another Freedom Foundation seminar.

At one of the seminars, S. Robert Lichter spoke about the survey he and Stanley Rothman had conducted in 1979 and 1980. They talked with 240 high-ranking journalists and broadcasters; their survey found that those making the decisions about what news will be covered overwhelmingly identified themselves as liberals and had voted for the Democratic candidate for President in all elections since 1964. [Appendix F contains a flyer distributed in the early 1980s which summarizes the survey findings.] The Lichter and Rothman study very much agreed with the conclusions I had come to as early as the late 1960s and early 1970s about the "media elite." ³

One of my prime reasons for wanting the national network news programs (the national voice of the media elite) to be available as widely as possible was that I felt that research and study would reveal why the country was changing its moral direction. Today, I feel that if historians and sociologists wish to try to determine why the vast social and other changes took place in the United States from the 1960s to today, they can get the answer from studying the television news programs available at the Vanderbilt Television News Archive. I think it is more than just a coincidence that the views of the media elite, as revealed by the Lichter/Rothman survey, became the most predominant views of many Americans from the 1960s to the 1990s. Had the media elite held the conservative views of the majority of Americans at the time this survey was made, I think the history of the United States would be vastly different.

The fact that the survey showed that the media elite was controlled by liberal Democrats helps to explain why the Democrats were in control of Congress for forty years. During those forty years, and until the advent of "talk radio" and its growth to the position it occupied with Rush Limbaugh and others in the early 1990s, the American people were almost completely dependent on the media elite for their knowledge of national and international affairs.

---

³ Lichter and Rothman conducted hour-long interviews with 240 journalists and broadcasters at the most influential media outlets, including the *New York Times*, the *Washington Post*, the *Wall Street Journal*, *Time*, *Newsweek*, *U. S. News and World Report*, and the news departments at CBS, NBC, ABC, PBS, and other public broadcasting stations. By "media elite" both they and we are referring to those people in the national news media who are responsible for making the important decisions about what news is shown and how. Appendix F shows a summary of the survey findings. The fact that the "media elite" believe as they do undoubtedly affects the beliefs of everyone in their organizations whose career progress is determined by these people.

The great growth of Rush Limbaugh and "talk radio" and the vast expansion of television news outlets weakened the hold of the media elite to a point which made it possible in 1994 for the Republicans to take control of Congress for the first time in forty years. Whether or not they will be able to retain and expand this control, facing the opposition which they will face from the media elite, the Democrats, and the bureaucracy, remains to be seen.

The Lichter/Rothman report caused me to remember again the feeling I had back in 1963, when President John F. Kennedy was assassinated in Dallas, Texas. I remember how distressed I had been at the fact that the national media, particularly television, continuously said that Kennedy's assassination was caused by the conservative atmosphere in Dallas at that time. They continued making this statement even after it was well-established that Lee Harvey Oswald was not a conservative and that the "atmosphere in Dallas" had nothing at all to do with the assassination. I wondered if this placing of the blame for the assassination of a popular President at the door of the conservatives was at least partly responsible for strengthening the liberal Democratic control of Congress, which lasted for forty years.

During this forty-year period, conservative Republicans were able to elect Presidents by raising enough money on a national basis to run paid commercials on network television to partially offset the fact that they did not receive as favorable coverage by the media elite. Most of the conservative Republican candidates for Congress did not have the financial ability to offset the liberal Democratic news media reports with paid commercials to present the other side. During this period of time, the liberal Democratic news media was constantly referring to conservative Republican advertising as "negative advertising." These advertisements were frequently "negative" only in the fact that they presented additional information (or sometimes different information) about the liberal Democratic candidates supported by the news media—many times information which should reasonably have been furnished by the news media.

The difference in the viewpoint of the media elite was, I think, clearly shown by the difference in the way they referred to the assassination of President Kennedy in Dallas and the attempt to assassinate President Ronald Reagan in

Washington, D. C., in 1981. As stated, they referred many, many times to the assassination of President Kennedy being caused by the "conservative atmosphere in Dallas." When the assassination attempt on President Reagan occurred in Washington, I do not believe there was ever the first reference to this attempt being caused by the liberal atmosphere in Washington, D. C.

I was meeting with Chancellor Heard, Fred Friendly, and others on the afternoon of March 30, 1981, when the assassination attempt was made. At that time, three television monitors were kept running all the time in the equipment room at the Archive so that Ron Moulton could be alerted to any breaking news. When the first report of the assassination attempt appeared on television, three recorders were immediately put into operation to record the news reports from all three networks. At the same time, someone from the Archive came to the place where we were meeting to tell us about the assassination attempt and the fact that they were recording the network reports.

Later, Fred Friendly and I were together and I remember specifically saying to him that I hoped and believed the networks would not blame the assassination attempt on President Reagan on the liberal atmosphere in Washington in the same way they had continuously blamed the assassination of President Kennedy on the "conservative atmosphere in Dallas."

I wish very much that the Archive had been in operation in 1963 as it was in 1981, so that the news reports about the Kennedy assassination could also have been recorded for posterity.

Mr. Lichter's presentation at the Freedom Foundation seminar reminded me of these thoughts, and I enjoyed his talk as well as both of my visits to Valley Forge very much.

After attending the seminar at Valley Forge in 1982, I went to Philadelphia and talked with Merrill Panitt, who was editorial director of *TV Guide* and was also connected with the Annenbergs, who at that time owned *TV Guide*. I never met Ambassador Annenberg, but I met with Panitt, who was very close to the Ambassador, several times to talk about funding for the Archive. We did receive a $100,000 matching grant from the Annenberg Fund, which was to be spread over three years.

I was very interested at this time in making educational presentations similar to the ones I made at Valley Forge. I, therefore, wrote a memorandum, a portion of which is printed below, to explain the presentation to others who might be interested.

MEMORANDUM
October 27, 1982

Walter Cronkite, the dominant figure in network television news in the 1970s, [4] is quoted in *The Atlantic Monthly* of January, 1981, as having expressed concern in 1977, to the Radio and Television News Directors Association, about the nature of television news:

> "We fall short of presenting all, or even a goodly part, of the news each day that a citizen would need to intelligently exercise his franchise in this democracy. So as he depends more and more on us, presumably the depth of knowledge of the average man is diminished. This clearly can lead to a disaster in a democracy."

In an interview reported in Parade, March 25, 1980, Cronkite is quoted as saying:

> "We need courses, beginning in junior high, on journalism for consumers. How to read a

---

[4] In fact, Walter Cronkite was the dominant news personality and anchor man through most of the 1960s, 1970s, and 1980s. During that time, CBS, whose news program was anchored by Cronkite, was the leading news network. (Author's comment, 1995)

newspaper, how to listen to the radio, how to watch television. How the news is gathered. Where the possibilities for error and opinion are. People have got to be taught to be skeptical of any single news source so that they won't become cynical about all news sources." [5]

Following fifteen years devoted to assuring the videotape recording of the network evening news programs and a continuous study of these programs, I believe Mr. Cronkite is correct and that efforts should be made to do what he suggests.

Believing that it is not enough to "talk about" news but that it is necessary to combine "talking" and "showing" to explain television news properly, I have prepared a 60 minute tape. This videotape contains 25 items that were selected to do what Mr. Cronkite suggests. . . .

It seems to me that Mr. Cronkite's recommendation could be carried out . . . on college campuses throughout the United States and . . . at luncheon clubs or other meetings.

---

[5] I think Cronkite realized very strongly that nobody should rely just on the Cronkite evening news—or any one source—for their coverage of news. Yet, one of the reasons I felt the tapes for the network news programs should be made available for study was that all of the polls and studies showed that the American people were doing just that—relying on the network news— and usually just one network—as the sole source of their information about national and international events. Because all the programs come on at the same time, there's no easy way to compare what ABC or NBC said to what was said on CBS. (Author's comment, 1995)

In order to do this, I am willing to devote any time and effort (within the energy resources of a 70 year old man) needed. I am willing to spend $5000 + to convert the [videotape] to 16 millimeter film. This appears to be advisable because many places do not have videotape viewing facilities but do have facilities for 16 millimeter film.

I did make a presentation of this nature to several groups of students in Nashville, and it seemed to be well-received. I also spoke at several luncheon club meetings but soon discovered that the "energy resources of a seventy-year-old man" were being overworked. Also, I came to the conclusion that so far as the club meetings were concerned it was too difficult to arrange for enough playback equipment and monitors so that the audience could see. I also came to the conclusion that television viewing, in 90% of the cases, consisted of one or a very small number of people in one room watching a small screen. I realized that it would not be the same with film on a large screen for a large audience. So far as educational classes were concerned, I felt that the presentation was simply too long and would be successful only where viewing equipment was already available and a small part of the tape could be shown at one time. Therefore, I didn't continue making presentations of this nature but turned my attention to other matters connected with the Archive's work.

It seemed as if we'd no more than finished celebrating the ten-year mark at the Archive than we were facing our fifteen-year anniversary. We had a luncheon celebration for the staff and their spouses, along with Chancellor Emeritus Alexander Heard and the new Chancellor of Vanderbilt, Joe B. Wyatt. I made a few remarks about those who had helped to make the Archive a reality.

Chancellor Emeritus Heard and Chancellor Wyatt also spoke briefly. Jim Pilkington had the final word and read a witty poem he had written entitled "Thoughts Cursory on an Anniversary." The poem opened with these lines:

> In '68 they made the decision
> To haul off and tape "The TELEVISION."
> Sometimes the tapes were a trifle hazy,
> And people all thought the tapers were crazy.

Even those of us closely involved with the Archive probably thought we were crazy a time or two, but as we looked back over fifteen years, we felt a great sense of pride in all that we had accomplished.

Chapter Seven

An End and a Beginning

W e had been interested for some time in expanding the services of the Archive to increase its visibility and use, and our discussions about new initiatives became more serious in 1984. Besides increasing visibility, we also felt that expanding our services could strengthen and solidify the Archive's fund-raising capacity. In addition to funding support from the Scaife Foundation, the Pew Memorial Trust, and the Justin and Valere Potter Foundation, we also received a grant in 1984 from the Mobil Oil Foundation. Vanderbilt wanted to expand fund-raising efforts, and someone from the fund-raising office was assigned to take specific responsibility for the library, including the Archive.

We were still working toward forming a National Board of Visitors, and we wanted to involve this board in considering new initiatives and funding options. However, we felt that some new services did not need to await the formation of this national board. In February, 1984, Jim Pilkington, Malcolm Getz, and I, along with several others, met with Chancellor Joe B. Wyatt to talk about a number of ideas. Getz had recently become executive director of the Vanderbilt Library. He was a firm supporter of the Television News Archive and contributed greatly with advice and support.

Four possibilities were discussed at the meeting:

1) A series of institutes or workshops for local station news directors.

2) The possible cataloging and dissemination of information about the Archive's special holdings, including such things as Watergate.

3) A seminar on the general subject of analyzing television news for Vanderbilt faculty.

4) A seminar on the archiving of television news in connection with the Library School at Peabody.

Although we continued to discuss these ideas, nothing specific had been done about these four proposals by the time of my retirement a year later.

We scheduled the first Board of Visitors meeting for November of 1984. Representatives from both ABC News and NBC News agreed to serve on the board, but CBS declined our invitation. The board also had members representing other media organizations as well as members representing academic institutions and major Archive donors. The board was interested in a variety of new initiatives for the Archive, including putting the index on computer, revising the price structure, and more aggressive marketing of the Archive's services. There was also a feeling that the Archive should make a more concentrated effort to gain assistance from the networks. There was extensive talk about this at board meetings. I think the Vanderbilt fund-raising office felt that the support of the networks was crucial to their efforts to secure significant funding from other sources.

Because of my history with the Archive and the networks, I strongly believed that the networks were never going to have favorable feelings toward the Archive as long as I was associated with it, so I then decided that it was time for me to leave. I certainly didn't object to the Archive receiving help from the networks—I'd been trying to get help from them since 1968. But I didn't think the Archive would ever get any assistance from the networks, particularly without any strings attached. If the networks did give assistance, I felt that they would want to put conditions on how the materials could be used.

I resigned as unpaid administrative consultant and member of the Administrative Committee effective February 15, 1985. I received letters of appreciation from a number of people, including Alexander Heard, Patrick Buchanan, Jeff Carr, Malcolm Getz, and Pat Wilson. The Board of Trust recognized me at a luncheon held in April and presented me with a silver tray inscribed with these words: "Presented to Paul C. Simpson, founder and creative force of the Vanderbilt Television News Archive, 1968-1985, with the deep appreciation of the Board of Trust of Vanderbilt University, April 26, 1985." There was also an article about me in the April 5, 1985, issue of the *Vanderbilt Register*.

When I resigned, I made it clear that if the people at Vanderbilt ever wanted to call on me for assistance, they could. I did have quite a bit of contact with Jim Pilkington while he was still there as administrator. I probably visited the Archive at least once a week during this time, and talked with Jim on the phone more frequently. Jim died in November of 1987, about six months before his scheduled retirement, and after that I didn't have any extensive contact with the Archive.

Since I was no longer a volunteer administrative consultant with the Archive, I felt free to express some of my own personal opinions about television news. During the period I had been actively involved with the Archive, I had refrained from making any critical comments about network news because of fear it might be detrimental to the Archive's work. I had refused several invitations to appear on talk shows. In the spring of 1986, I felt free for the first time to accept an invitation to be a guest on a local radio talk show. I enjoyed my visit very much and felt that the talk show host also enjoyed our discussion. We talked primarily about the media, and several times the host said something to the effect that "we could talk with Paul Simpson about this forever" and that listeners could be sure I'd be back. Well, I never was invited back, and I think I know why I wasn't. The station didn't want to be critical of the networks, and some of my comments clearly were. As a former television anchor person said to me, "there was no law against news media criticizing news media—it just wasn't done."

1986 was a busy year for me personally, and it was also a busy year for the Archive and Vanderbilt. In the spring, ABC came to Vanderbilt to do a "Viewpoint" broadcast. They first contacted me about coming to Vanderbilt. They said the Archive was one of the reasons they chose Vanderbilt as a broadcast site.

Since it became clear to me that radio as well as television were going to be unavailable for me to express my opinions about network coverage of various issues, I decided in 1988 to write several articles for the "Community Voices" column of the *Nashville Banner.* [Examples in Appendix G] I did not continue this writing as it was too complicated since I had to write the articles in longhand, have them typed by a public stenographer, reviewed and corrected by me, and then retyped and submitted to the paper. Also, around that time both my wife and I developed health problems.

The Archive celebrated its twentieth anniversary on August 28, 1988. The celebration was attended by Chancellor and Mrs. Joe B. Wyatt; former library director Frank P. Grisham; Luann Pilkington, Jim's widow; Jean and Alexander Heard; the newly-named director of the Archive, Scarlett Graham; and me. The *Nashville Banner* also printed an editorial congratulating the Archive on its twenty-year anniversary and wishing it continued success.

In 1989 and 1990, the Archive received grants from the National Endowment for the Humanities, the National Science Foundation, and the National Historical Publications and Records Commission. These major grants helped the Archive continue its work transferring the reel-to-reel tapes to cassette and developing an electronic database. The Archive had also by this time revised its fee schedule to try to recover more of the actual costs of operation and negotiated an arrangement whereby the Library of Congress would compensate the Archive for providing copies of tapes for its collection.

The Archive continued to prove itself to be of significant value, with the television industry itself being the second-largest group to use the Archive (academics were the largest group). Over the years, the Archive has served a wide variety of organizations, and numerous diverse publications have made use of Archive materials.

An example from the 1980s illustrates clearly to me the importance of the Archive's collection. When the hostages were released from Iran, the State Department asked the Archive to prepare a tape of specific items to reorient the hostages after their release. Someone prepared a list of items and asked the Archive to prepare the tape. The tape was used when the hostages stopped over in Germany on their way back to the United States, and it was also used during their stay at Annapolis. I thought this activity was a very interesting use of the Archive, showing recent history to an unusual group because they had been cut off from that history.

Despite the problems over the years, I feel a great sense of accomplishment in knowing that the Archive collection now documents history going back more than a quarter of a century. Although partial collections of news programming now exist elsewhere, the Vanderbilt Television News Archive remains the world's most extensive and complete archive of television news. Perhaps *Variety* best summed up the value of the Archive in an April 5, 1972, article: "The astonishing aspect of the Vanderbilt project is that it is the only storehouse of the evening news shows. In an age dominated by television news, it is only the Nashville school that is providing historians with source material."

The most recent years of the *Index and Abstracts* are available on the Internet, and work continues to make available electronically all the years back to the 1968 beginnings. In this manner, the collection has been accessed by people from all fifty states and every continent except Antarctica. The Archive typically has about 2,000 requests per year that translate into roughly 1,000 tapes on loan at any given time in forty-five states and five to seven foreign countries. To fulfill these requests, the Archive's current staff of eight draws upon the more than 24,000 individual ABC, CBS, and NBC network evening news broadcasts and 8,000 hours of special news programs such as the Watergate hearings, the Gulf War coverage, the Democratic and Republican national conventions, CNN's *Prime News*, and ABC's *Nightline*. The networks themselves have often called upon the Archive for tape of past events, and although they have never given any on-air publicity to the Archive, the networks are clearly aware of its importance. According to a story in the November, 1991, issue of *Texas Monthly* magazine, CBS anchorman Dan Rather said he lives with two burdens—the ratings and the Vanderbilt Television News Archive.

Each evening, the Archive's collection grows as videotaping off the air continues.

CONCLUSION

I n reflecting on my experiences with network television news and the networks themselves and my other experiences in Washington, New York, and elsewhere, I have come to some conclusions about what has taken place in this country since 1968. These conclusions are also based on a great deal of thought given to this matter over many years. I am sure it is possible that these conclusions are not completely correct, but I do think they are of sufficient importance to deserve the consideration of as many people as possible.

I believe that beginning in the 1960s it became important to many people for this country to leave the type of government set up by the Founding Fathers. This type of government called for the leaving of all government activities possible as close to the people as possible—through the local and state governments. The Constitution and the Bill of Rights make that principle reasonably clear. For example, Amendment X of the Bill of Rights states, "The powers not delegated to the United States by the Constitution, nor prohibited by it to the States, are reserved to the States respectively, or to the people."

However, in the 1950s and 1960s, a number of things happened which changed the perception of this principle. First, there were a number of liberal, Democratic desires that could not be passed by the local and state government because too many of the voters did not want them. A decision was then made that the best way to have these passed was to take them away from the people and remove them to Washington. In Washington, special interest groups could have significantly more influence on the votes, and the public at large would not have the same impact.

At the same time, an interesting development occurred. California Governor Earl Warren had been a possible candidate for the Republican nomination for President when he withdrew in favor of Dwight D. Eisenhower, who was later nominated and elected as President of the United States in 1952. Shortly after Eisenhower took the oath of office, Warren was nominated by Eisenhower and approved by the Senate as Chief Justice of the Supreme Court of the United States in 1953. Later, Warren is reported to have said that he, as Chief Justice of the United States, would have a greater effect on the history of the United States than Eisenhower would as President.

If he made this statement, he was undoubtedly correct. Earl Warren did have a much greater impact on the United States as Chief Justice of the Supreme Court, a position he occupied from 1953 to 1969, than Eisenhower ever had as President. The reason for his impact is that Warren presided over one of the most active Supreme Courts that this country has ever had—that is, the most active in writing law rather than interpreting law. He and his court, which he controlled to a great extent, took the position that they had the power —and they used this power—to interpret law in the way that they wanted to interpret it rather than trying to simply interpret law from the standpoint of what the framers of the United States Constitution intended. They, in effect, "wrote laws." This action resulted in more and more people seeing their ability to control their lives in many important matters being taken away from them and their local and state government and transferred to lifetime federal judges who are not elected by the people.

At the same time, the liberal Democrats came to power in Congress. Those people in favor of a "liberal" agenda felt that if they could get their agenda transferred to Washington, they would get a favorable decision from either the Supreme Court or the Democratically-controlled Congress. They felt that the Supreme Court would interpret the law in a way that they favored. If they chose to advance their agenda by legislative action, they felt that they could more likely have desired legislation enacted by a liberal, Democratic Congress in Washington, D.C., than by local and state governments which were much closer to the voters. This course resulted in more and more power being shifted from the local and state governments to the federal government in Washington.

At about the same time, national television networks came into existence and started telecasting from three networks the main information that the public had about national and international affairs. All three networks were headquartered in New York City, in the same liberal atmosphere, and soon came to adopt and promote the same liberal "point of view" on social, political, and moral issues. Therefore, the United States had in Washington a liberal Supreme Court and a liberal Democratic Congress and in New York the liberal "media elite" of the national news media, all pushing for the liberal agenda. [Appendix F, a summary of the Lichter/Rothman survey of the "media elite."]

The media elite built for themselves enormous power by having everything concentrated in Washington. The networks already had television broadcast facilities and staff there and were able to have other people bring matters to Washington for them to report. This contributed to even more power being concentrated in Washington. Many, many things that the founders of this country would never have thought of being decided by the federal government were taken away from the local and state governments and transferred to the hands of the federal government.

It was also easy for the networks to have national impact because they were, as a former president of CBS was quoted as having said at one time, "the only national daily press" that this country had. The people who ran the "national press," the media elite, therefore, secured for themselves enormous prestige, power, and pay and were able to push their point of view by showing the American people what they wanted to show them and by not showing them what they did not want them to see. They controlled most of what the American people saw and heard about national and international affairs and as a result had a tremendous impact on setting the agenda for the United States.

In a way, what happened was similar to what happened at the Democratic Convention in Chicago in 1968. For a reason which prevented them from broadcasting live coverage—the telephone strike—the networks set up cameras and lights at the corner of Balboa and Michigan, believing that if they set up television cameras and lights there, the demonstrators would come there. By the same token, the media elite, particularly national network television, found that if they had in Washington an easy way to telecast live the events of this nation, then a great many more of the events of this nation would come to Washington so that they would be televised and have their influence.

It would not have been possible for the three networks in this country to develop the control they developed over national news reporting if it were not for the fact that so many of the government decisions became concentrated in Washington. The networks could not in any way have given the same coverage nor had the same amount of influence if the decisions had been made by numerous local governments and fifty state governments. It would have been impossible for them to have had the same prestige, the same power, and the same pay and to be able to push their point of view in the same way that they were able to do by having everything concentrated in Washington.

Perhaps the definitive example of the power of the media elite came during the mid-1970s. My intentions when I started this book were to leave out any references to Watergate because it had been such a controversial subject. For years it was "politically incorrect" to say anything positive about President Richard Nixon or his administration or to raise any questions about what happened at Watergate or what happened in the impeachment attempt of President Nixon. However, as I was finishing the book, I realized that it was simply too important a period of time during the life of the Archive not to be covered. I also realized that the way this series of events was covered by national network television clearly illustrated the power of the networks.

First, Watergate probably received the most extensive media coverage of any event that the Archive has recorded in its existence. The Archive has numerous tapes of the reporting of the original Watergate incident as well as the Senate and House hearings. The Watergate tapes have probably been more requested than any other tapes in the Archive over the years. One of the tapes that has been particularly requested is the tape of President Nixon's farewell speech to his staff.

I prepared a tape for showing to the Board of Visitors in which I included the original coverage of the break-in at Watergate. The audience laughed when the narrator, in telling about the break-in at the Watergate office of the Democratic National Committee, ended by saying something to the effect that "we will probably hear more about this."

We did, of course, hear a great deal more about it. The news media and the media elite seized upon this incident as an opportunity to help them do what I think they had wanted to do for some time, remove Richard Nixon as a political force in the United States. In this effort, the media elite had the assistance of the bureaucracy, as Nixon had stated in his 1972 election campaign that if reelected he intended to do something about reducing the size of the bureaucracy. They also had the full support of the Democratic Congress at that time.

There are a number of questions about the Watergate break-in itself which I hope I live long enough to have answered. I think the American people will learn the answers only when it is no longer "politically incorrect" to say anything good about Nixon or to raise any questions about the accepted "facts" of Watergate. I have over the years been intrigued by the fact that the break-in was, without any doubt, not known about in advance by President Nixon. There has been no one who has charged otherwise.

Another point that intrigues me is that someone involved in the break-in operation is reported to have taped the door into the Democratic office with tape across rather than up and down the door in such a way that it could not easily be seen by anyone who would be passing the office. He surely knew better than to do it that way. However, he did it that way anyway, apparently for the reason of wanting to be sure the tape was noticed. He put the tape across the door in such a way that the night watchman in the Watergate building saw the tape and took it off the door. For some reason, the night watchman did not report this incident to the police at that time (or at least we were not told that he did). When the person who had taped the door discovered that the tape had been removed, he put the tape on the door again in the same manner, apparently so that it would undoubtedly be noticed by the night watchman during his rounds. He must have known better. He must have known that he could tape up and down rather than across the door so that it would not be noticeable by anyone passing the office door.

The night watchman later, in the middle of the night, discovered the tape the second time, and this time reported it to the police. We're told that, by a strange coincidence, two police officers who were not normally in that area at that time and who possibly would not have been in the area the first time the tape was discovered were in the area and responded to the report of the break-in.

It is also interesting that the members of the group who broke into the office had large-denomination bills in their possession. These were easily traceable to the White House. Apparently, someone wanted the break-in to be discovered, and that someone also wanted the money in the possession of the people who broke in to lead back to the White House. This series of events, of course, occurred and started the whole episode of "Watergate."

We were never really given any clear information as to what was hoped to be gained by the break-in. There are still a great many questions in my mind as to why the Watergate break-in occurred in the first place and particularly why it was apparently deliberately set up in such a way as to be discovered and investigated by the two policemen who "just happened" to be in the area in the middle of the night to respond to the call from the night watchman when he removed the tape the second time.

For weeks, all of the network television coverage about any misconduct on the part of anyone in the Nixon administration would be reported under a headline "Watergate." This approach was used even when the actual episodes would have nothing whatever to do with the break-in at Watergate or any effort by the administration to cover up the incident. For example, the question of "dirty tricks" during the campaign—the question of any misconduct of any kind on the part of anybody in the administration—would be reported under the banner of "Watergate."

I think we can understand the impact of that labeling if we consider what would have been the impact on the American public if within the past year or so everything reported on any of the trouble with the Clinton appointments or any of his administration officials had been reported on television under the heading "Whitewater." The American public were encouraged to tie questions about any kind of misconduct on the part of anybody in the Nixon Administration to "Watergate," in a way that they have not been encouraged to tie questions about any misconduct in the administration of Clinton to "Whitewater."

In February of 1973, the Senate voted to establish a select committee, chaired by Senator Sam Ervin, to hold public hearings to investigate charges of corruption. The entire hearings were telecast to the American people. One of the interesting things that happened during this procedure was the day a secretary had testified about Nixon's activities. One of the news commentators had just finished stating that it was very clear from Senator Howard Baker's comments and demeanor that he had doubts about the secretary's testimony. Unfortunately for the television commentator, at that point Senator Baker arrived. When asked about his opinion of the secretary's testimony, he praised it very highly. This example again emphasized to me that when we are told something by a television commentator, we are not told of it as *his opinion*, but are told of it in such a way that we are encouraged to think of it as factual, when, as shown in this particular instance, it is not.

The news media's constant reference to any misconduct under the headline of Watergate and the desire of the bureaucracy to remove this President who had said during his campaign that he was going to make every effort to reduce the size of the bureaucracy, plus the desires of the Democrats, who then had control of Congress and had had control for years, to emphasize a "scandal" involving a Republican president, led to the bringing of impeachment charges against Nixon in the House of Representatives.[1] The House Judiciary Committee began an inquiry in December of 1973 and ultimately voted three articles of impeachment in July, 1974.

---

[1] Watergate undoubtedly contributed to the election of a Democratic President, Jimmy Carter, as well as to the election of numerous Democratic members of Congress in the next election.

The news media "bragged" constantly about the fact that the American people were for the first time able to see on television the full proceedings of a committee in taking strong actions against a President of the United States. What the news media did not say was that the Democratic majority on the committee, which fully controlled its actions, would meet in "closed door" sessions in advance to determine each day what would take place in the open hearings shown on television. Any decisions of any importance would be made behind closed doors, and then the American people would see on television what had been carefully scripted for them to see and hear. We were never shown any of the meetings behind closed doors.

There are a great many other issues involved in the Watergate matter, including the appointment of a special prosecutor and Nixon's efforts to have him removed, all of which were covered fully by television. The fact was that Nixon decided he had no alternative but to resign as President of the United States. This he did on August 9, 1974.

His speech to the American public was reported on television, as was his farewell speech to the White House staff. These are among the most requested tapes in the Archive. A number of Watergate studies used tapes from the Archive. I do not know whether or not these studies were actually completed and a full report made to the American public. I do know that if these studies were completed they were not covered on network television news—at least not to the extent that I knew about it, and I watched a lot of television news at that time, as I still do.

The full Watergate tapes are available at the Archive at Vanderbilt. My hope is that one day someone will do a complete investigation of the entire matter but will do so only after it is no longer "politically incorrect" to say anything good about Nixon or his administration. I also hope the study will be reported on network television or on national radio talk shows, which are now giving the American people an alternative source of information.

I think history is going to repeat itself now on the Watergate affair, to some extent. Newt Gingrich and the Republican Congress have the same opponents that Nixon had, except that there is now a Democratic President instead of a Democratic Congress. It will not be exactly the same, as history is seldom exactly the same, but one can certainly see some idea of what may happen in the future by seeing what has taken place in the past.

In my opinion, what is going to happen and is happening in this country now, is that the media elite, their Democratic friends in Congress and the administration, and the bureaucrats, are not going to be happy with the Republicans having control of Congress and having the ability to reduce the size of the Washington bureaucracy and take away from the media elite a great deal of their prestige, power, pay, and ability to emphasize their point of view. The media elite, along with the others, have a tremendous interest in seeing to it that the Republican "Contract with America" does not succeed and that the Republicans do not succeed in transferring power from Washington to the local and state governments.

There is another reason why the media elite did not like the results of the 1994 election and does not look forward to any further movement in the direction pointed out by the 1994 election. Over many years the media elite and their carefully-selected and controlled assistants in Washington have been able to establish both social and business relations with leaders of the liberal Democratically-controlled Congress and the liberal Washington bureaucracy. It is very distasteful to them to now have to relinquish those contacts and try to establish new contacts in order to obtain "inside information" for use in their news programs. Besides it being a difficult job for them to establish these new contacts, they would not have the same "liberal" contacts that they had before.

The media elite and the national network news departments are probably going to do everything that they possibly can to see to it that the Republicans and their "Contract with America" are not successful and to see to it that power remains concentrated in Washington. The Washington bureaucrats, of course, will attempt to do the same because they will wish to keep their jobs. The Democratic President will not object to this process because he will hope that eventually, with the news media support and the bureaucratic support, the Democrats will again take control of Congress just as they had control for forty years.

It is most important that the American people understand the present situation and try to see to it that power and responsibility is transferred from Washington back to the local and state governments, where the people themselves can have something to say about what is done. If power is transferred from Washington and the federal government to the local and state governments, the local television stations will then begin to operate as they did prior to the advent of the three national networks. They will report on national and international as well as local affairs from a point of view which will probably be different from station to station. The point of view will certainly not be as one-sided as it is now, concentrated in the hands of three networks headquartered in the same liberal atmosphere in New York. Technical developments have made it possible for the local stations to do more than serve as a "conduit" for the national networks.

Fortunately, the situation is different today from what it was at the time of Watergate, as there are more sources of news today. Also, the advent and growth of talk radio (especially Rush Limbaugh) has developed a situation where the American people are not completely dependent on the three networks and the media elite for their knowledge of national and international affairs. The three networks and the national newspapers that comprise the media elite are no longer in a position to completely control what the American people see and hear about what is happening today.

However, since television is still one of the major sources of information in our country, it is my hope that readers of this book will become more skeptical of what is presented to them as "fact" on the network news programs. There are a number of ways the viewer may determine when a program is not presenting a balanced viewpoint. When one sees a panel of three people discussing a particular topic, such as the "Contract with America," and two of them are very clearly on the liberal side and only one is on the conservative side, it is obvious that the program is not being even-handed. This is particularly true when the network news moderator's questions or comments obviously indicate his liberal viewpoint as well. When the moderator asks questions of one side and then "cross-examines" the other side, the viewer can get a pretty good idea of which side the media favors. It is also an indication of wanting to favor a particular viewpoint when one side is allowed to make lengthy opening remarks, as well as closing remarks, and the other side is permitted to make only a short opening statement, with no closing statement at all.

The television viewer must always remember that the media elite have a list of prominent people and national leaders indicating what their particular viewpoints are. The networks can at any time present the viewpoint they want presented by asking a person with that viewpoint to appear on the program and by not asking someone with the opposing viewpoint to appear. One of the strongest tools that the liberal media has is the ability not to show to the American people that which they do not want them to see. Until the advent of talk radio and C-SPAN on television, it was extremely difficult to try to find out what it was that the network news programs had not shown. I know because I have visited libraries and studied newspapers and magazines trying to find out what actually happened that I was not told about by the network news. Fortunately, with talk radio and with other sources of news available today, it is much easier to see how the media elite try to influence news by not showing certain events or not giving air time to certain people to discuss these events.

In addition, the media have learned from experience that some people with a particular viewpoint that the media doesn't favor will present such a weak argument that they ultimately bolster the opposing perspective. If a network shows a supposedly "balanced" presentation, with one person strongly supporting the point of view that the media favors and the other person opposing that point of view, it will frequently feature a person to present the opposing view who they know from experience does a weak job.

It is important that the American people understand that they can expect a barrage of criticism of the conservative viewpoint and of the Republican proposals and the "Contract with America." The media elite will try to preserve their prestige, power, pay, and ability to express their point of view. Also, the bureaucrats will make every effort to keep their jobs and the liberal Democrats will try to regain control of Congress. The American people must become concerned and skeptical viewers, keeping in mind that the networks rely on conviction, controversy, and a particular point of view and that the news presented on television each day is not necessarily complete and factually correct. They must be willing to be steadfast and to remember that they can express their opinions through talk radio and C-SPAN, through the voting booths, and through the wider variety of news media that are now available.

Appendix A

Proposal for Television Library Project

There is widespread controversy about television's impact on the American people. Indeed, in this year of social unrest, heated political debate, and international crisis, the television networks have been variously and sometimes haphazardly referred to as instigators of or catalysts to the social change taking place in this nation.

The Nielsen survey of October 1, 1968, estimated that viewers of the half-hour Walter Cronkite news program (CBS) numbered 16,370,000, that 14,230,000 saw the simultaneous Huntley-Brinkley Report (NBC), and that 6,920,000 viewed the Frank Reynolds news program (ABC).

The total of 37,520,000 for all three network news programs is considerably below their peak; the number of television viewers increases during the fall and winter months. (The total U.S. Population according to the U.S. Census two years later in 1970 was 203,302,031.)

There are very remarkable aspects of this reliance by some thirty or forty million Americans on television for daily news capsules. Many of the viewers depend exclusively on the medium for their impressions of the world beyond their neighborhood. Furthermore, a long-range Roper poll reported last summer that television is now the nation's primary news source and that the public places greater faith in what is shown on television than what is printed in newspapers.

Yet, despite the wide viewing audience and the increasing influence of this news medium on the American people, television news broadcasts are not being preserved on videotape for study in future years. . . .

. . . America is, therefore, losing forever a unique record of the historical events of our time as well as a prime source for research by psychologists, sociologists, political scientists, economists, and historians. It is difficult to imagine the loss that would accrue if, for example, copies of the *New York Times*, which are kept routinely by virtually every library in the country, were destroyed two days after publication. And just as libraries maintain newspapers and magazine collections, technology now permits the acquisition and maintenance of television news broadcasts and other programs of current and historical interest. For a history-making and history-conscious nations, this oversight in the television medium is an anachronism of almost inconceivable proportions. Indeed, the American people are probably unaware that these records are not being kept somewhere. . . .

The total budget for the (current) three-month (experimental) period is $18,685. This figure does not include any charges for management, professional consultants, or housing of the material. With the assistance of these interested donors (Massey, Wilson, Vanderbilt University, and myself), the original three-month project has been financed, but sustained follow-up coverage will be lost if additional support is not obtained immediately.

Because of this project's historical value and its potential use in identifying the impact of television on American attitudes and behavior, ultimately perhaps on our national and international destiny, Vanderbilt University feels strongly that the project should be continued. The university, therefore, proposes to extend the project for three years. The main objectives of such an extended test are the following:

1. To record for posterity a resource now being lost.

2. To develop a precise methodology for content analysis of the telecasts, drawing upon the many relevant academic disciplines in the Vanderbilt University community.

3. To develop a classification and indexing system to manage the wealth of information that will be collected.

4. To work with electronic equipment manufacturers to perfect the taping process and develop inexpensive copies of master tapes as well as subject-matter tapes for wide use in academic and other institutions.

5. To provide this information perhaps through automated retrieval systems with a minimum of inconvenience to scholars and researchers.
6. To demonstrate through this test that a national agency such as the Library of Congress could and should take over this task on a permanent and continuing basis.

Once master tapes of news broadcasts are secured, subject-matter tapes can be produced from them. This process will permit, for example, scholarly investigations of what the national networks were reporting on the Vietnam War while the Paris peace talks were in session, or what effects television had on a third party Presidential candidacy. In addition, videotapes could be made from the master tapes for educational use in high schools, public libraries, or academic libraries and by civic clubs and continuing education centers. The possibilities are abundant, but the primary need is to secure the basic sources of information, the master tapes.

Total costs for the three-year period are budgeted at $370,755. Initial equipment expenses will be $54,975, and operation expenses will amount to $105,260 per year. A substantial portion of the annual operating expenses is devoted to the analysis and indexing processes which will provide the persuasive evidence that the project is both feasible and worthy of continuation. Developing systems for easy identification and access and developing the methodology for content analysis will make the tapes operational for a multitude of research projects. This budget is modest for a program of such vast scope, but Vanderbilt is hopeful that the three-year demonstration will show the way for a more appropriate repository whose resources would permit expansion of the project's full potential on a national and international scale. Vanderbilt feels a particular responsibility for this program because no other group or agency in the nation seems willing to take it on just now and because such an encouraging start has been made in the three-month trial period. Vanderbilt is convinced that an investment in this program will provide support for an historical collection of significance for generations to come.

Appendix B

VTNA Index and Abstracts
March 12, 1971

5:55:50   COMMENTARY (JAPAN IMPORT SETTLEMENT)

          (S) Japan textile ind. negotiated import settlement with   HKS
          Reb. Wilbur Mills instead of admin.; Nixon vetoed agreement.
          Situations reflects problems of US Govt. System; British
          Govt.System runs smoother.

5:57:50   GOOD NIGHT

Friday	March 12, 1971	CBS

5:30:10   INTRODUCTION   WALTER CRONKITE (NYC)

5:30:40   LAOS / TCHEPONE

          (S) SVN forces withdraw from Tchepone, Laos area;   WC
          US copters airlift 1000 SVN from Fire Base Sophia, Laos.

5:31:20   Nixon / Eisenhower

          (S) David Eisenhower graduates from Naval Officers School; WC
          Pres. Nixon addresses graduates.

          (Newport, RI) Construction ind. & anti-war protesters kept   Dan
          at distance.(Nixon - says US must maintain strength to keep   Rather
          cherished values; understands arguments of new isolationists;
          understands cost of weakness.) Film shows Nixon presenting
          diploma to David Eisenhower.

5:33:50   (COMMERCIAL: Pontiac; Alberto V05.)

5:34:50   MIL. CORRUPTION HEARINGS

          (S) Sen. Abraham Ribicoff says late Rep. Mendel.Rivers   WC
          attempted blocking Col. Earl Cole's investigation.

          (DC)[RIBICOFF - asks Cole how Wm. Crum's name engraved with   David
          others on cigarette box, presented to Gen.Westmoreland, if Schoumacher
          Cole didn't know Crum.] [COLE - says Crum asked
          secy. to have name added to box.]   Cole denies 26 alleged
          instances advancing Crum interests. [COLE - says talked
          with Rivers, who set up phone call between Cole & Ribicoff
          concerning investigation.] [RIBICOFF - says Rivers attempted
          to block investigation, but failed; says received several
          calls from Rivers on Cole's behalf.]

5:38:10   HERBERT / NVN POW MISTREATMENT

          (S) Strong reaction to Lt. Col. Anthony Herbert charges of   WC
          NVN POWs mistreatment.

          (Ft. McPherson, GA) [HERBERT - says most common reaction   Foster
          is that it's time story made public, but don't think will   Davis
          make it.] Herbert charging both POW's mistreatment &
          superior ofr.'s cover-up.

5:39:30   POWS / CROSBY

          (S) Bing Crosby & associates rptdly.attempting negotiation   WC
          ransom for US POW's in NVN.

5:39:50   KISSINGER / CO-CONSPIRATORS

          (S) For. Affairs Adviser Henry Kissinger met privately with 3   WC
          co-conspirators in plot to kidnap him; participants quoted
          describing meeting amicable, bitter-sweet.

5:40:20   CA / UN-AM. ACTIVITIES CMTE.

          (S) CA Subcmte. on Un-Am Activities abolished after   WC
          Sen. Ldr. James Mills finds name in Subcmte.'s files.

5:41:00   (COMMERCIAL: Sears Laundry Detergent.)

5:42:00   TURKEY / PREM. RESIGNATION

          (S) Turkey mil. demands resignation of Prem. Suleyman   WC
          Demirel or face coup; Demirel resigns.

5:42:30   N. IRELAND / BELFAST

          (S) Protestant & Catholic shipyard workers march together in   WC
          Belfast, N. Ireland demanding terrorism crackdown in wake
          of killing 3 British soldiers.

5:42:50   MIDDLE E. / FULBRIGHT / USSR

          (S) Sen. Fulbright says USSR agreed to participate in Peace   WC
          Keeping Force, if Israel & Egypt reach agreement.

5:43:10   USSR / SPACE PROGRAM

          (S) USSR rptdly. resuming program to land cosmonauts on moon.   WC

5:43:30   APOLLO 15

          (S) Apollo 15 astronauts use vehicle to move on moon.   WC
          (Taos, NM) Film shows astronauts practicing with lunar rover.   Richard
                                                                            Threlkeld
          (Kent, WA) Actual vehicles built in Kent, WA, at cost of   Bill
          $10 million a piece.   Stout

5:45:20   SEN. / SOCIAL SECURITY

          (S) Sen. approves Social Security incrs., 10-56%.   WC

5:45:50   BURGER / CT. REFORM

          (S) Chief Justice Burger proposes both sides of ct. case share   WC
          litigation costs to prevent bluffing until last moment before
          negotiating settlement.

5:46:20   FTC / MORRIS ADS

          (S) FTC goes to ct. to stop Philip Morris Corp. from   WC
          distributing Personna Razor Blades as ad samples in Sun.
          newspapers.

5:46:50   (COMMERICIAL: Tums; Absorbine Jr.)

5:47:50   SEAL SLAUGHTER

        (S) Rptr. warns viewer film scenes of seal slaughter in Canada   WC
        unpleasant.

        (Grindstone Is., Canada) Film shows seals clubbed to death;   Ike
        controls sealpop., protects fishing ind. [Intl. Fund for   Pappas
        Animal Welfare Spn. Brian DAVIES - says this yr. clubbing more
        brutal than ever.] [Zoologist Dr. Keith RONALD - says clubbing
        death least painful method.] 50,000 seals killed in 4-5 days.

5:50:50   BIG BEN

        (S) London landmark has maintenance problems.   WC

        (London, England) Frederick Dent firm informs govt.   Bob
        terminating contract to service Big Ben. [Dent Chrm. Geoffrey   Simon
        BUTCHER - says men able to handle upkeep of Big Ben retired,
        died or left for other jobs.] [Clock Mechanic Bill ELSON - says
        Big Ben gains or loses time depending on temp.; pennies placed
        on pendulum correct time.] BBC uses Big Ben chimes to begin
        newscast; Dent firm conts. maintenance until alternative found.

5:54:30   CHICAGO / CONVENTION CMTE.

        (S) Chicago, IL, Mayor Daley appts. cmte. to bid for both Demo.   WC
        & Repb. 1972 conventions.

5:54:40   UAW / STRIKE

        (S) UAW employees strike for higher wages.   WC

5:55:00   STK. MKT. RPT. (S)   WC

5:55:20   (COMMERCIAL: Star-Kist Tuna.)

5:55:50   NIXON / INTERVIEW REACTIONS

        (S) Women rptrs. expect news conf. with Pres. Nixon; only 9   WC
        selected to interview Pres. about wife's upcoming birthday.
        [Women's Wear Daily Rptr. Candy STROUD - says news controlled.]
        [NY Daily News Rptr. Ann WOOD - Says Pres. must not know what
        botched up job exists between him & media.] [El Paso Times Rptr.
        Sara McCLENDON - says Pres. wife doesn't need Nixon press conf.
        to build her up.] [STROUD - says only allowed to ask permitted
        questions.] [WOOD - says specific ground rules for interview.]
        [McCLENDON - says Pres. should talk to all rptrs., not just
        those writing sweet story about him.]

        (S) Hell hath no fury. . . .   WC

5:57:40   GOOD NIGHT

FRIDAY   MARCH 12, 1971   NBC

5:30:10   INTRODUCTION   FRANK McGEE (NYC); JOHN CHANCELLOR (DC)

5:30:20   TURKEY / PREMIER / RESIGNATION

        (s) Turkey Mil. Ldrs. demand Prem. Demirel's resignation;   FM
        Demirel resigns.

        (Ankara, Turkey) Pol. ldrs. must find more conservative,   Douglas
        authoritative Prem.to satisfy mil.; no tension from events;   Kiker
        kidnapping 4 USAF men fatal blow to Demirel Govt.

        (s) Kidnappers wanted more liberal govt.   FM

5:32:30   MIDDLE E. / PEACE PROPOSALS

           (s) Israel presents new peace proposal to UN Mediator   JC
           Gunnar Jarring; US pressuring Israel to accept US proposal
           for UN Peace Keeping Force. (State Scy. ROGERS - says Admin.
           hopeful of Middle E. agreement; explains US plan for UN Peace
           Keeping Force.] (Sen. FULBRIGHT - says USSR has agreed to
           participate in Peace Keeping Force.]

           (DC) US trying to convince Israel position not compromised   Richard
           by withdrawal from occupied territory; move leads to peace   Valeriani
           agreement assured by Peace Keeping Force. US discusses econ.
           aid & mil. commitment to Israel in exchange for cooperation now.

5:35:20   (COMMERCIAL: Williams 'Lectric Shave.)

5:36:10   HERBERT / VN CIVILIAN MISTREATMENT

           (s) Lt. Col. Anthony Herbert files derelection of duty   JC
           charges against superior offrs. in VN Offrs. failed to
           investigate torture & murder of VN civilians.

VANDERBILT
Television News Archive

The Vanderbilt Television News Archive, administered through the Joint University Libraries of Vanderbilt University, Peabody College, and Scarritt College, maintains a videotape collection of the evening newscasts of the three major television networks—ABC, CBS, NBC. Begun in August, 1968, this collection is added to daily as these news programs are broadcast from local stations in Nashville, Tennessee. Although network television newscasts are generally known to be the major source of national and international news for most Americans, complete videotapes of the programs are note being permanently saved elsewhere. The cost and technical problems at present are greater by far than those faced when libraries routinely maintain files of daily newspapers, but the purpose is the same: to preserve a record of today for the usefulness of that record tomorrow and later.

Characteristics of the Collection

At present, the collection consists of more than 3,000 hours of news programs, with at least seven and a half hours added each week. The collection includes some additional material, such as Presidential speeches, political conventions, Watergate hearings, and the like. The tapes are available for study, either within the Archive or through rental of the tapes for use outside the Archive. Charges depend on the extent of use and service, and on the relationship of the user to the three institutions sponsoring the Joint University Libraries.

A system of indexing and abstracting the tapes has been developed to facilitate access and reference to the collection. Abstracts for years 1968 to 1972 are available for use in the Archive.

In March, 1972, the Archive began publication of a monthly index to television news, entitled *Television News Index and Abstracts*. The first number was for January, 1972. The index is combined with abstracts of the news programs as broadcast in Nashville, Tennessee, during a given month. It is currently being published on an experimental basis and circulated without charge to selected libraries, institutions, and individuals. After a trial period, it is the intention to continue this publication as a subscription item. Microfilm of the publication for the year 1972 is available for $120.

Background of the Archive

At the onset, August 5, 1968, the Archive—created on the inspiration of a Nashville insurance executive and Vanderbilt alumnus, Paul C. Simpson—was financed by grants from Nashvillians Jack C. Massey and David K. Wilson, the Massey Foundation and the Justin and Valere Potter Foundation. This initial funding chiefly provided for the purchase of raw videotape and the rental of recording machines. There was no regular staff until April of 1970, which meant that many hours of recordings were made and added to the collection identified only by network and date, without notation of content.

In January, 1971, the original founders were joined by others, making possible the purchase of more sophisticated recording equipment and the design of an indexing system, with a small staff for this and administrative purposes. Grants are being received from these and other sources.

Administration

The Archive is directed by a three-man committee named by the Chancellor of Vanderbilt University on authorization of the executive committee of the University's Board of Trust. Chaired by Robert A. McGaw, secretary of the University, the committee includes Frank P. Grisham, director of the Joint University Libraries, and Mr. Simpson, the originator, who serves as administrative consultant. James P. Pilkington is the administrator.

In addition to the administrative committee, a University committee serves in an advisory relationship on academic matters.

Characteristics of the Recordings

The master recordings of the program are made on Ampex one-inch helical-scan videotape recorders. These tapes, recorded on lo band, are playable on all Ampex one-inch helical scan video recorder/players. Copies are also available for 1/2 inch EIAJ-1 players, and 3/4 inch U-matic cassette players.

Since January 1, 1971, the videotape of each program has been marked, in the recording process, with the initials of the network, the date of the program, and the Nashville time (at ten-second intervals) of the receipt of the image from the air. This information is superimposed on the program picture as the programs are recorded, greatly facilitating reference and particularizing documentation for studies based on the collection. The equipment used for making the recordings likewise has the capability of producing compiled, or subject-matter tapes. These can be made on order, subject, of course, to appropriate charges. Audio cassettes of programs may also be rented.

Terms of Use

Within terms of Archive policies governing charges and restrictions pertaining to public showings, rebroadcast of the materials, and duplication of the tapes, the material may be rented—unaltered and as aired—either in complete programs or as compiled subject-matter tapes. No material is sold, and none can be duplicated or rebroadcast. Basic rental charges are as follows:

$30 per hour of compiled material
$15 per hour of duplicated material
$ 5 per hour of audio-only material

with a half-hour minimum charge. Tapes rented for use elsewhere than in the Archive require deposits on the materials used. These are refunded when the tape is returned in reusable condition. Material deposits are:

$50 per hour of one-inch tape
$35 per hour of duplicated material
$25 per hour of half-inch tape
$ 1.50 per hour of audio tape

Viewing charges at the Archive are based on $2.00 per hour of viewing machine use.

To date, authors, graduate and undergraduate students, professors, television station personnel, and public officials have used the collection.

VANDERBILT TELEVISION NEWS ARCHIVE
Joint University Libraries
Nashville, Tennessee 37203
Telephone: (615) 322-2927

Appendix D

Statement of
Paul C. Simpson
Before the Subcommittee on Courts, Civil Liberties,
and the Administration of Justice
of the
House Committee on the Judiciary
Supporting the retention in H.R. 2223 of Section 108 (f)(4)
and the words "other than an audiovisual work dealing
with news," in Section 108(h).
June 12, 1975

Mr. Chairman and Members of the Subcommittee:

I am Paul Simpson of Nashville, Tennessee, and am appearing here today as an individual citizen at my own expense. I have, for over seven years now, been interested in the fact that network television news is recognized as the most important source of information about national and international affairs. I have, therefore, believed that it should be retained as broadcast and made as easily and readily available as technology permits, for research, review, and study, both now and in the future. Since learning in 1968 that these broadcasts were not being retained at the networks or elsewhere, I have devoted a great deal of time to this matter.

In 1968, I was instrumental, financially and otherwise, in the establishment of the Vanderbilt Television News Archive at Vanderbilt University in Nashville, Tennessee. This has been and is the only existing archive of videotapes of all three network television evening news programs.

I have read with great interest the attached page S16162 of *Congressional Record-Senate* of September 9, 1974. [Appendix F] I would like to endorse the remarks of Senator Howard Baker as reported on this page and request permission to include this page S16162 as part of my statement.

I favor not only the passage of a copyright bill that would not prevent Vanderbilt from doing what it is doing in its television news archive operation but also one that would not prevent any library in the country from doing the same. I recognize that it is probable that costs involved by the present state of technology make necessary one or two collections of network television news open for use on a national basis. Because the expense involved makes it financially unlikely that there will be many such collections, it is important that the tapes in these collections be as readily and easily available as possible.

This, in turn, makes it imperative that any collection now established or that may be established by congressional action or by library action not be thwarted by the copyright law in making this material available to the public for reference, research, and study. The proliferation of video tape recorders and players will make—and in many instances already has made—it as reasonable for a library user to view video tape material in his home as for him to read a library book there, or a copy of a library newspaper there. The copyright law should not prevent libraries making television news material as easily and as conveniently available as they make other such news material available from the library. With regard to television news as with other library news materials, if the original copy cannot be taken away from the library, the library should be free to make copies for the user to use away from the library. The user should be free to obtain individual news stories and news items from a television news collection as he is to get copies of news stories and news items from newspapers in the library.

To permit the copyright law to be so revised as to be useful in blocking public access to old television news broadcasts would be an injury to the public interest.

That the public has the right to see old television news broadcasts— "old" meaning those already aired—is substantiated by publicly-granted privileges which, if withheld, would make the existence of television news impossible. For a very small fee, television stations are licensed by the public to use the publicly-owned airwaves. Because the airing of news via television is deemed to be for the public good and in the public interest, television stations are required by law to air news broadcasts. The news broadcasters are granted exceptional privileges, even by proposed H.R. 2223 itself. For example, copyrighted materials such as books, newspapers, and magazines may be quoted and otherwise used in "news reporting" with or without permission of the copyright holder under Section 107 of H.R. 2223. Other privileges are extended. For example, newsmen, including television newsmen—with their lights and their cameras—are permitted access to publicly-owned property, denied to the average citizen, (certainly an individual equipped with camera and lights) in order to gather the news. To have, then, an exclusive-rights copyright that would, in effect, deny the average citizen access to these news stories as televised, (after being televised at a profit to the network) except with the express permission of the broadcaster, does not seem to be proper.

To summarize, the newly-revised copyright legislation should not prohibit libraries from

1.   Recording news broadcasts from the air.
2.   Making them available for viewing at the library and copies for viewing elsewhere.
3.   Making, on specific request, copies of single stories or news items from the broadcasts available, just as such services are rendered by libraries from newspaper collections.

These privileges should be granted to libraries and the users of libraries for the following reasons:

1.   Television news broadcasts are too significant as a record of the times, not to be retained as aired.
2.   Broadcasters themselves have traditionally not retained these programs.
3.   Libraries are beginning to recognize their own obligations in this regard.
4.   Television news is now being recognized by scholars as significant source materials.

5.   Television news is broadcast for the public good and in the public interest.

6.   Television broadcasters enjoy privileges granted by the public which makes television news possible.

    a. Right to use airwaves

    b. Exemption from copyright restrictions on material used as part of "news reporting."

    c. Access to and freedom of use of public property, including installation of such equipment as lights and cameras, which is denied the average citizen but which is granted the newsman to assist him in performing his work of gathering the news.

Libraries should have the same right to collect and circulate television news broadcasts that they have traditionally had to collect and circulate copies of newspapers and other forms of print journalism. The revised copyright law should not abridge this right of the libraries and so of the general public.

For these reasons I urge the retention in H.R. 2223 of section 108(f)(4) and the words "other than an audiovisual work dealing with news" in Section 108(h).

Thank you for the privilege of appearing before you.

Appendix E

Proposal of Advisory Board for
The Vanderbilt Television News Archive

June 2, 1980

Consideration should be given to the establishment of a National Advisory Board for the Vanderbilt Television News Archive. This idea has been discussed from time to time in the past, but for several reasons has not materialized. Among these reasons has been a feeling of impermanence of the Archive. I believe this should be disregarded, as a Board could be established even for the short duration of a few years.

Except for the rendering of services from the existing twelve-year collection, the future of the Television News Archive really can never be projected beyond a few years into the future. Changing technology itself contributes to a certain impermanence of procedures. The development of the videodisc, for instance, which should make possible the widespread distribution of news broadcasts on discs, at low cost, could render it no longer necessary for the Archive to build its collection by off-air taping. Cable TV will also have an impact on distribution of the news.

Despite changes of this type, however, Vanderbilt must recognize the continuing necessity for the Archive to render services nationally and internationally. Considering this, it seems reasonable for the Archive to have a National Board of Advisors.

This board would meet at least once (perhaps twice) a year at Nashville to review the operations of the Archive, make suggestions for its future operations, and advise about on-going funding.

Toward the establishing of the board, there should first be a meeting of Chancellor Heard, President Fields, Sam Fleming, and Pat Wilson to consider the matter. If they react favorably to the idea, they could then begin the process of selecting prominent business people, political figures, and educators to serve on the board. It is fortunate that there are living in Nashville, and in the state of Tennessee, many persons who meet all the requirements. Perhaps there should first be a meeting of those persons from Nashville and elsewhere in Tennessee, with later the addition of others from various places in the United States. (The Scaife interests should be involved in the process from the outset.)

Among questions that could be explored by the board would be expansion of the Archive's collections (addition of the morning news, for instance) and finances of the on-going present operation. (Suggestion: seek ten, twenty-five, or fifty corporations or foundations who would give annually and proportionately to comprise the Archive's basic operating budget of $250,000.)

In order to accomplish this goal, it would be imperative that Vanderbilt University, Chancellor Heard, President Fields, Sam Fleming, and Pat Wilson commit their tremendous prestige and influence to compel first, local and state leaders, described above, and then national leaders, to visit the Archive to become thoroughly familiar with its purpose and operation and to become convinced that the Archive's activities are necessary. For the next several years, these activities will not be continued unless Vanderbilt does so.

Appendix F

Media Elite Out of Step
With the American Public

A 1980 survey appearing in *Public Opinion* magazine, a publication of the prestigious American Enterprise Institute, details dramatically why President Reagan's conservative program is under such attack in the media.

It shows how out of step with average Americans the media elite actually are.

The authors of the survey conducted hour-long interviews with 240 journalists and broadcasters at the most influential media outlets, including the *New York Times,* the *Washington Post,* the *Wall Street Journal, Time, Newsweek, U.S. News & World Report,* and the news department at CBS, NBC, ABC, PBS and other public broadcasting stations.

Here are just some of the highlights of their findings:

** Ideologically, a majority of leading journalists describe themselves as liberals. Fifty-four percent place themselves to the left of center compared to only nineteen percent who choose the right side of the spectrum.

** When they rate their fellow workers, even greater differences emerge. Fifty-six percent say the people they work with are mostly on the left and only eight percent on the right—a margin of seven to one.

**   Looking at their voting records in Presidential elections from 1964 to 1976 (the survey was taken before the 1980 elections, of those who say they voted, the proportion of leading journalists who supported the Democratic presidential candidate never dropped below eighty percent.

**   In 1972, when fifty-two percent of the electorate chose Nixon, eighty-one percent of the media elite voted for McGovern.

**   In 1976, leading journalists preferred Carter over Ford by exactly the same margin—eighty-one to nineteen percent.

**   In 1968, eighty-seven percent backed Humphrey over Nixon, while in 1964, media leaders picked Johnson over Goldwater by the staggering margin of sixteen to one, or ninety-four to six percent.

**   Most significant, though, is the long-term trend. . . . In an era when Presidential elections are often settled by a swing vote of five to ten percent, the Democratic margin among elite journalists has been thirty to fifty percent greater than among the entire electorate.

**   In 1978, seventy-eight percent earned at least $30,000 and one-third earned over $50,000.

**   Geographically, two-thirds come from that quadrant of the country extending from New England to Chicago's North Shore. By contrast, only three percent are drawn from the entire Pacific Coast, including California, the nation's most populous state. Some forty percent of the media elite come from just three states: New York, New Jersey, and Pennsylvania.

** A predominant characteristic of the media elite is its secular outlook. Exactly fifty percent eschew any religious affiliation. Another eleven percent are Jewish and almost one in four (twenty-three percent) was raised in a Jewish household. Only one in five identifies himself as a Protestant and one in eight as Catholic.

** Only eight percent go to church or synagogue weekly and eighty-six percent seldom or never attend religious services.

** Virtually half, forty-nine percent, agree with the statement, "the very structure of our society causes people to feel alienated.". . . Twenty-eight percent agree that America needs a complete restructuring of its basic institutions.

** Leading journalists emerge from our survey as strong supporters of environmental protection, affirmative action, women's rights, homosexual rights, and sexual freedom in general.

** Three quarters disagree that homosexuality is wrong and an even larger proportion, eighty-five percent, uphold the right of homosexuals to teach in the public schools. (A mere nine percent feel strongly that homosexuality is wrong.)

** On foreign policy, the media elite is similarly liberal. Fifty-six percent agree that American exploitation has contributed to Third World poverty. About the same proportion, fifty-seven percent, also find America's heavy use of natural resources to be 'immoral'—a common Third World charge against the U.S.

Given these liberal convictions on the part of the people who filter and then write most of the news reports the public receives, how can they expect conservatism to receive a fair shake? Or President Reagan and his programs?

As columnist Patrick Buchanan noted after reading the results of the media elite survey, the most serious problem of conservative governments is "How to sustain public support for your policies when those who daily report, explain, and analyze them are in profound disagreement?"

Appendix G

The media role as 'adversary'

By Paul Simpson
Special to the Nashville Banner

The massive coverage given by U.S. television to the Reagan-Gorbachev summit emphasizes the relevance of the following "observations" written some years ago. Network evening news programs shown in the United States tonight will be seen via satellite in the world tomorrow. A former president of a network news department indicated that "'conviction, controversy and a point of view" were essential to a successful (presumably in terms of audience secured) news show. This has proved to be eminently correct and has resulted in "controversy" being a very important and sought-after part of all television news.

Simpson

Perhaps this explains why our country has been torn apart by controversy and why it becomes increasingly difficult for any administration or Congress (democratic or Republican) to govern the country.

In the 1970s it also became standard for news media, especially electronic, to indicate, at least, that their proper relationship with the United States government was that of an "adversary."

Webster's New World Dictionary defines adversary as "a person who opposes or fights against another; opponent; enemy."

Perhaps our country can survive if domestic and internal matters are reported to the people of the United States by a powerful news medium which emphasizes controversy and prides itself on being an "adversary" to our government.

We are now, however, well into a worldwide situation different from that ever faced before. Satellites have made possible and will expand even more the availability of worldwide instant communication.

COMMUNITY VOICES

There is no question that the United States has very powerful enemies in the world. Communications and their use have become and will become even more a vital part of the conflict. It is better for this conflict to turn on communications than on war.

We would not think of facing a military conflict with our Army, navy and Air Force controlled by people or forces that emphasize controversy with our government and consider themselves as "adversaries" to the government. Can we accept without consideration a situation that results in our worldwide communications being controlled by persons and forces who emphasize controversy and state their position is that of an "adversary" to the U.S. government?

There is no question that almost without exception our world enemies understand the power of communications and consider control of the means of communications as important as control of their army, navy and air force. Whenever a change in government takes place almost anywhere in the world, particularly by coup or revolution, the first step of the new government is to take over the control of the news media.

It seems to me that there must be some middle ground between government control of the news media and control of the media by those who emphasize controversy and proudly consider themselves "adversaries" to the government.

Since the United States came into existence, we have had weapons and powerful explosives controlled by our military forces. We did not consider it necessary to require that these explosives be placed under the president's sole control. When atom and hydrogen bombs were developed, however, we did not take the positions that these were just other weapons, other explosives. We rightly said that they were not, that they were so much more powerful that they deserved great considerations and new "rules." We therefore considered and then established those new rules.

When television came in there was a tendency to treat it as "just another news medium." Insufficient consideration was given to new "rules" for this new form of communication in view of its great impact.

With respect to television, we are now proceeding with the development of satellites, into a completely new situation. There has never been a time, and probably never will be a time, when any print medium will have the ability to go worldwide. Pictures, however, can be seen and understood anywhere; there is no language barrier.

Are we going to make the mistake of treating this entirely new situation by the "old rules," or are we going to say as we did when the nuclear bombs were developed that we must consider and adopt "new rules?"

I very strongly believe that the existence of the United States depends on our giving careful consideration to the questions raised in these observations. I am convinced that I know the "question." I am sorry to say that I am *not* convinced that I know the "answers." I am convinced that the answers must be aggressively sought and by as many people as possible and as soon as possible.

Vice President George Bush is our second highest elected official and one of only two American leaders selected in a national election.

If so little respect is shown to him and his position by Dan Rather, how can foreign viewers of CBS evening news have any respect for the United States or its leaders? The CBS news of Jan. 25 was shown via satellite, to the world the next day.

Paul Simpson is a former mayor of the city of Oak Hill and former administrative consultant and founder of the Vanderbilt University Television News Archives.

NASHVILLE BANNER
Forum Section

Appendix H

Accuracy of political polls doubted

By Paul Simpson
Special to the Nashville Banner

Do we really want our government run and its leaders determined by polls sponsored and published — or not published — by the "national media"?

The "national voices" of the "national media" and the most prominent members are ABC, CBS and NBC.

How many of us have ever been contacted by one of these polling organizations?

Simpson

How many of us have refused to participate in these telephones polls? Who are those who do participate? Are they representative of the country as a whole, or are they, as a group, much more likely to be activists and to have certain, perhaps distinctive belief — i.e., desire a big and bigger federal government?

What percentage of those called who do participate in opinion polls are knowledgeable about the subject on which they are expressing an opinion? A poll on supporting the "freedom fighters" or "Contras" — giving financial aid to them — revealed that only 39 percent knew that the Reagan administration was supporting the Contras. The others either thought the administration was supporting the Nicaraguan government or simply did not know whom it was supporting.

When Congress votes against aid to the Contras or on any other issue is it unduly influenced by incorrect or uninformed polls sponsored by and reported on by the "national media"?

Are presidential candidates taking positions based on erroneous and unreliable polls? Albert Gore, Jr., in remarking

COMMUNITY VOICES

on Richard Gephardt's strategy, recently stated, "It is possible in this day and age to poll and learn what resonates with the voters. You can then take those poll results and mold your campaign to them."

Why do we place great value on the secrecy of the voting booth and then allow important decision s to be based on non-secret telephone polls? Certainly the number called is not a secret and therefore it is easy to determine to whom the telephone number belongs. This may cause many people not to participate or to give what they believe to be the popular opinion.

Are polls even reasonably accurate? Unfortunately for the public, there is no way to determine the accuracy of current opinion polls. The only polls whose accuracy can be judged are those made and reported on before an actual election. Most of these polls have turned out to be inaccurate.

An example of this inaccuracy was demonstrated during the New Hampshire primaries, especially the Republican election. The polls taken immediately before the election either showed George Bush and Bob Dole even or Dole ahead. One of the best-known and most prominent polls gave Dole and 8-percent-point lead. When the actual voting took place, Bush won 38 percent to 29 percent over Dole.

> **Are presidential candidates taking positions based on erroneous and unreliable polls?**

All of the preceding remarks have been addressed to the problems which could exist even if the poll was made honestly, professionally, objectively and with no effort to word the questions or the order of the questions in such a way as to get a desired result.

There is, however, an even greater potential problem with polls. A polling organization has been quoted as asking before a poll was conducted what result was desired. It indicated that the result desired could be secured by the order and wording of the question asked.

If our government leaders and policies adopted are going to be greatly determined or affected by polls, should not consideration be given to setting standards for poll-taking? Among other standards, should information be required as to the number and percentage refusing to participate; how many were knowledgeable about the subject; what the actual questions were, and in what order they were asked?

If this is not done would not the country and its welfare best be served by the news media continually alerting the American people to the possible danger of relying on polls? The New Hampshire results show that simply stating a small figure as a possible percentage of error is not enough.

Paul Simpson is former administrative consultant and founder of the Vanderbilt University Television News Archives and a former mayor of the city of Oak Hill.

NASHVILLE BANNER
3/8/88
Forum Section

Appendix I

TV advantage goes to Gorbachev

By Paul Simpson
Special to the Nashville Banner

As the time for the Moscow summit approaches it is appropriate to review the television networks' coverage of the Washington summit in December 1987. We can then compare how President Reagan and Mikhail Gorbachev were covered in Washington and how they could be covered in Moscow.

Simpson

There were and will be very important differences. Gorbachev was able to severely restrict coverage in Washington, and will be in Moscow. Reagan did not have this ability in Washington and will not be permitted either by Russia or by the networks themselves to have it in Moscow. This must affect the coverage so as to favor Gorbachev.

To demonstrate Gorbachev's ability to control and restrict coverage even in Washington, consider the following:

All Gorbachev's meetings and press conferences in Washington were held in the Soviet Embassy compound. Gorbachev furnished all camera persons and directors, who were therefore completely controlled by him. The American and world television viewers were not informed of this.

Admission to the compound was completely controlled by Gorbachev. The networks had to accept this or run the risk of not being able to cover at all. The networks would not accept such control by Reagan.

COMMUNITY VOICES

On the final day of the Washington summit Gorbachev invited Vice President George Bush to breakfast in the Russian compound. Bush was kept waiting for about one hour. We were not told by the networks that Gorbachev did this and that he did it because some negotiations were not going as he desired. This mad Gorbachev and Bush an hour late leaving for a meeting with Reagan. Even so, Gorbachev, on his own, stopped his car and got out to speak with some Americans.

These actions of Gorbachev made him about 90 minutes late reaching the White House. When he did, Reagan was shown on television saying to him, "I thought you had gone home." We were *not* shown Gorbachev's response: "I had a chat with a group of *Americans who stopped our car*" (emphasis added). Of course he himself had stopped his car, not the Americans.

We were also not told by the networks that Gorbachev had not informed Reagan that he would be late.

It is certain that the American network news coverage would have been extensive and extremely critical if Reagan had deliberately kept the second-highest Russian official waiting for an hour, then had kept Gorbachev waiting for 90 minutes, had not had the courtesy to inform him that he would be late, and then had lied about the reason for being late. Reagan would never have done that, but if he had the negative coverage would have been massive.

Gorbachev clearly had expert advice on how to manipulate American net-

works. He stopped his car to get out and visit at a busy corner where he knew television would cover his activities.

A "news conference" was scheduled for the afternoon of the final day. It was held in the Russian Embassy compound with all camera persons, directors and invitations controlled by Gorbachev. Gorbachev made a very long opening statement. It is clear that he and his advisers did not want the American people to see him answer questions even though he had carefully selected the journalists in attendance who could ask questions.

Apparently he was advised that TV stations throughout the United States would leave the press conference and not cover it if it ran into their local evening news programs. His advice was correct. Most local TV stations left the coverage before questions were permitted.

It is not possible that the American networks would have failed to report and comment unfavorably if this manipulation had been done by Reagan.

I very much hope that the American television networks will give equal and complete coverage of the summit in Moscow, even at the very real risk of being denied the right to cover Gorbachev or Russia now or in the future.

It is important that the people of America and the world see equal and complete coverage. Gorbachev and Russia should not be handed a communications and public opinion victory at the expense of Reagan and the United States.

Paul Simpson is former administrative consultant and founder of the Vanderbilt University Television News Archives and a former mayor of the city of Oak Hill.

NASHVILLE BANNER
Tuesday, May 24, 1988
Forum Section

INDEX

ABC 8, 10-11, 16, 27-28, 31, 38,72, 74, 89, 91, 100, 113, 129, 141-142, 147, 152, 154
Accuracy in Media (AIM) 103
Adolph Coors Foundation 127
Agnew, Spiro 48-49, 61-62, 64-65
Agronsky, Martin 33
American Film Institute 105, 107
American Television and Radio Archive 130
Ampex Corporation 21, 23
Annenberg, Ambassador 145
Annenberg Fund 145
Annenberg School of Communication 91
Associated Press 39, 49, 65
Atlantic Monthly 115, 146
Attica State Prison 90
Ayers 38
Baker Amendment 106-108, 117, 119-120
Baker, Howard 30, 44, 49, 52, 79, 95-96, 106, 109, 117, 129, 133,163
Bark, Dennis L. 93
Benson, Brien 93
Bergeron, Paul 20
bias 18, 24, 60, 78, 103
Bill of Rights 4, 157
Boorstin, Daniel 130-131
Brinkley, David 10, 18, 33
Broadcasting 24, 49, 102, 112
Brock, Bill 30, 44, 78
Buchanan, Patrick 44-45, 48-49, 53, 57, 104, 123, 153
Burger, Warren 62
Burleson, Aaron 66, 71, 83
C-SPAN 167
Campbell, Dr. Glenn 58, 93
Carr, Jeff 96, 99, 102, 133, 142, 153
Carrington, Frank G. 89-90
Carter, Jimmy 59, 163
Carthage Foundation 53, 58, 67, 70, 81-82, 97-98, 127
Catalano, Richard 9
CBS 2-3, 8-13, 16, 28-30, 35, 38, 52, 72, 74-85, 89, 91-93, 99-105, 107-112, 116, 119-116, 120, 125, 129, 133, 139, 142-143,146-147, 152, 156, 159
Chicago 21-24, 160
Clinton, Bill 162-163, 165
Clouse, Wilburn 59

CNN 155
Columbia University 8, 22, 60
Columbus Dispatch 127
conservative 5, 17, 60, 66, 143-145, 166-167
Contract with America 3-4, 195-167
controversy 2, 4, 6, 35-37, 39, 42-43, 61, 66, 78, 122-123,135-137, 139-140, 167
conviction(s) 2, 6, 35-36, 38, 42, 66, 78, 123, 135, 139-140, 167
Copyright Bill 114
Copyright Law 130
Copyright Office 82, 135
Cronkite, Walter 1, 10, 38, 41, 77, 99, 104, 107, 147
Dallas 5, 144-145
DeFranco, Joseph 91
Democrat(s) 4-5, 21-23, 28, 36, 43, 48, 54-56, 72, 88, 109-110, 121, 125, 136, 143-144, 155, 158-161, 163-165, 167
Department of Defense 9, 41
Department of State 19, 41, 155
DeWitt, John 20, 51, 71
Dole, Robert 74, 78
Drinan, ? 115-117
Earheart Foundation 128
Eckhardt, Bob 48
Eisenhower Commission 44, 48
Eisenhower, Dwight D. 158
Election 1968 21-22, 24, 87
Election 1972 98
Election 1976 121, 123-125
Election 1994 3, 165
Erlick, Everett 27-28, 141
Ervin, Sam 163
Ervin, Thomas 29
Evans, Robert V. 28-30, 83-84, 108, 114
Evening Star 79
Fairness Doctrine 91, 112
Federal Communications Commission 3, 9, 12, 18, 24, 30, 45, 89, 91,117
Fern, Alan 31
Fields, Emmett 20
Fleming, Sam 58, 131-132
Ford Foundation 8-9, 22-23, 95-96, 107, 127-128
Foundation for American Communications 134

Frank, Reuven 52, 79, 91
Freedom Foundation 142, 145
Freeman, Leiper 20
Friendly, Fred W. 2, 6, 8, 9, 22, 34-36, 66, 96, 123, 141, 145
Fulbright, William 33
Fulton, Richard 30, 44
George Peabody College 59, 71, 75, 152
George Washington University 129-130
Getz, Malcolm 152-153
Gingrich, Newt 164
Glenmeade Trust 141
Goodman, Julian 28
Gore, Albert Sr. 30
Graham, Scarlett 154
Grisham, Frank 9, 20-21, 31, 52, 54, 71, 89-90, 96, 99, 132, 154
Gulf War 155
Hagerty, James 31
Hansen, Clifford 74, 77, 78
Hardacre, Paul 20
Heard, Alexander 9, 20, 22, 52-54, 59-60, 83, 96-98, 92-94, 100, 102,130-131, 133, 141, 145, 148, 153, 154
Hoover Institution 58, 93
Hoover Presidential Library Association 90
Hewlett Foundation 141
Hume, Jacquelin 58
Humphrey, Hubert H. 24
Huntley, Chet 10, 18, 38
Internet 155
Iran hostage crisis 155
Irvine, Reed 103
Jackson State College 60-63
Jenkins, George 27
Johnson, Lyndon B. 3
Johnson, Nicholas 18, 30
Joint University Libraries 9, 52, 54, 64, 71, 75, 81, 89, 132
Kastenmeier, Robert 108, 112-115, 117-119
Kennedy, John F. 5, 144-145
Kent State University 60-63, 92
Kirby, John J. 64
Kuiper, John 30
Laos 74, 71, 78
Larry, Dick 93, 129
Leary, Timothy 7

ABOUT THE AUTHORS

PAUL C. SIMPSON was a district manager with the Metropolitan Life Insurance Company in Nashville, Tennessee when he established the Vanderbilt University Television News Archive. The Archive he founded in 1968 encountered many obstacles, including a 1973 lawsuit by CBS designed to stop the archiving of important television news programs. This lawsuit was later dismissed when the new copyright law was enacted, not only providing for the Vanderbilt Archive to continue, but, of equal importance, effectively removing all restrictions and bans on the videotaping of television news by any library that met certain conditions. This ensured that television news could be on record for vitally important research and study, just as print news had always been. Brimming with anecdote, personal reflection, and eye-witness insight into some of the most momentous decisions of the twentieth century, *Network Television News: Conviction, Controversy, and a Point of View* is a refreshing behind-the-scenes look at one of the most important institutions in the modern world. From 1952 to 1985, Mr. Simpson served as commissioner, vice-mayor, or mayor in the Nashville satellite city of Oak Hill—the last seventeen years as mayor. A 1933 honor graduate of Vanderbilt law school, Mr. Simpson is retired and lives in Nashville with his wife Adelaide (Pod).

PATRICIA G. LANE is an anthropologist and writer in Nashville, Tennessee. A native of east Tennessee, Lane received a B.A. in English from Berea College and an M.A. in cultural anthropology from the University of Tennessee. She has worked as a newspaper reporter, a teacher, and a historical researcher. Lane is the author of several articles and one book, *Sweet Days, Precious Memories: A Brief History of the Hixson-Skymount Community.* She also served as the Deputy Director of the Tennessee Humanities Council for six years and currently edits its magazine *Touchstone.* Her interests are organizational history and issues of leadership in organizations.

After graduating from Florida State University with an M.S. in mass communications, **F. LYNNE BACHLEDA** worked at various PBS affiliates across the country to produce documentaries. She has been a freelance researcher and writer since 1981, working with national clients including *Time-Life.* Since that time she has worked with many national clients searching the Vanderbilt Television News Archive for important news information. She currently writes about religion for *Publisher's Weekly,* and works with museums to produce historical exhibits. At present, she is collaborating with The Tennessee State Museum as the historian for the Tennessee Bicentennial Capitol Mall that will commemorate 200 years of Tennessee statehood on June 1, 1996.